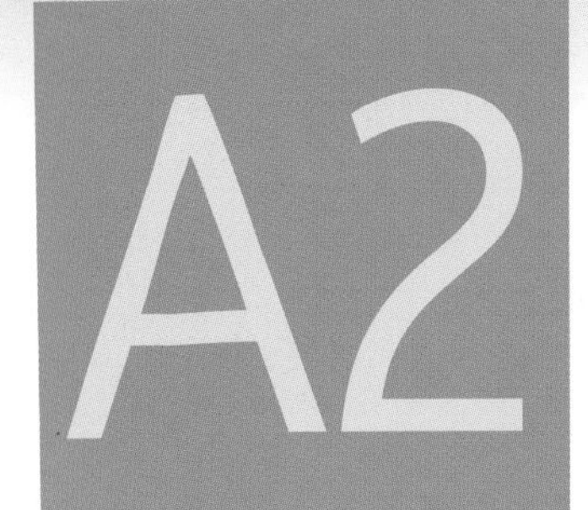


**Exclusively endorsed by AQA**

Adrian Beard
Pete Bunten

Nelson Thornes

Published in 2008 by:
Nelson Thornes Ltd
Delta Place
27 Bath Road
CHELTENHAM
GL53 7TH
United Kingdom

09 10 11 12 / 10 9 8 7 6 5 4 3 2

A catalogue record for this book is available from the British Library

ISBN 978 0 7487 8289 5

Cover photograph by Photolibrary/Digital Vision
Page make-up by Pantek Arts Ltd, Maidstone, Kent

Printed and bound in Croatia by Zrinski



**Acknowledgements**

The authors and publishers wish to thank the following for permission to use copyright material:

p2: © Waltraud Grubitzsch/dpa/Corbis; p7: © Construction Photography/Corbis; p14: © Blue Lantern Studio/Corbis; p20: © The Art Archive/Private Collection/Marc Charmet; p22: © Three Witches by Fuseli, Henry (Fussli, Johann Heinrich) (1741–1825) Collection of the Royal Shakespeare Theatre/The Bridgeman Art Library; p28: © The Art Archive/Museo del Prado Madrid; p46: © The Art Archive/Musée du Louvre Paris/Gianni Dagli Orti; p47: © ITV/Rex Features; p52: © The Art Archive/Museé du Louvre Paris/Alfredo Dagli Orti; p66: © Ceres by Bianchi, Pietro (1694–1740) Private Collection/Photo © Christie's Images/The Bridgeman Art Library; p73: © Donald Cooper/Photostage; p90: © Mary Evans Picture Library; p95: © Mary Evans Picture Library; p107 © Bettmann/CORBIS

Bite Me Magazine for an extract from 'Sweeney Todd is new dungeon "hair-raiser"', *Bite Me*, Issue 19 (2007) p7; Gordon Dickerson on behalf of the author for Tony Harrison, 'Remains' in *Collected Poems* by Tony Harrison, Penguin (2007); Faber and Faber Ltd for an extract from Philip Larkin, 'Going going' in *Collected Poems* by Philip Larkin (1990) and for Philip Larkin, 'Mr Bleaney' in *Collected Poems* (1988); David Higham Associates on behalf of the Estate of the author for extracts from Dylan Thomas, 'Fern Hill' in *Poems* by Dylan Thomas, J.M. Dent; The Orion Publishing Group for an extract from R.S. Thomas, 'A Peasant' in *Collected Poems 1945–1990* by R.S. Thomas, J.M. Dent (1993); Oxford University Press for the definitions of 'Gothic' in *Shorter Oxford English Dictionary*, eds Trumble & Brown (2002); and 'Pastoral' in Oxford English Dictionary, eds Simpson, J. & Weiner, E. (1989); Penguin Group for extracts from Sue Townsend, *Queen Camilla* (2006) pp3, 50–2. Copyright © Sue Townsend 2006.

Every effort has been made to contact copyright holders and we apologise if any have been overlooked. Should copyright have been unwittingly infringed in this book, the owners should contact the publishers, who will make corrections at reprint.

# Contents

# AQA introduction

Nelson Thornes has worked in partnership with AQA to ensure this book and the accompanying online resources offer you the best support for your A Level course.

All resources have been approved by senior AQA examiners so you can feel assured that they closely match the specification for this subject and provide you with everything you need to prepare successfully for your exams.

These print and online resources together **unlock blended learning**; this means that the links between the activities in the book and the activities online blend together to maximise your understanding of a topic and help you achieve your potential.

These online resources are available on kerboodle! which can be accessed via the internet at **http://www.kerboodle.com/live**, anytime, anywhere. If your school or college subscribes to this service you will be provided with your own personal login details. Once logged in, access your course and locate the required activity.

For more information and help visit **http://www.kerboodle.com**

Icons in this book indicate where there is material online related to that topic. The following icons are used:

### Learning activity

These resources include a variety of interactive and non-interactive activities to support your learning.

### Research support

These resources include WebQuests, in which you are assigned a task and provided with a range of web links to use as source material for research.

### Analysis tool

These resources help you to analyse key texts and images by providing questions and prompts to focus your response.

## How to use this book

This book covers the specification for your course and is arranged in a sequence approved by AQA. The introduction to the book explains what will be required of you as an English Literature student. There are two units in the book, the first of which, Unit 3, will prepare you for the examination. This unit is divided into Section A, which covers Elements of the Gothic, and Section B, which covers Elements of the Pastoral. Each genre is explored in detail, followed by an explanation of how to revise for and answer each of the two types of exam question.

Unit 4 is a guide to your coursework study. This unit takes you through advice on further reading, comparing texts, reading critical material, the critical anthology and preparing for the coursework submission.

Definitions of any words that appear in bold blue text can be found in the glossary at the back of this book.

The features in this book include:

*Aims of the chapter*

At the beginning of each section you will find a list of learning objectives that contain targets linked to the requirements of the specification.

### Key terms

Terms that you will need to be able to define and understand. These terms are coloured blue in the text book and their definition will also appear in the margin and in the glossary at the back of this book.

### Language hint

Straightforward definitions of terms that you may not have come across. These will help you understand less familiar words in the extracts within this book.

### Hint

Useful suggestions for study.

### Remember

Reminder of key terms and ideas that you have already come across earlier in the textbook.

### Links

Links to other areas in the text book which are relevant to what you are reading. Links can also refer you to longer extracts to be used in activities; these can be found in the Extracts section at the back of the book.

### Further reading

Suggestions for other texts that will help you in your study and preparation for assessment in English Literature B.

### Activity

Activities to develop skills, knowledge and understanding that will prepare you for assessment in your English Literature B course.

### Extension tasks

Tasks that take your learning further to increase your skills and give you even more knowledge and understanding, preparing you to demonstrate capabilities worthy of high grades. You should complete these activities when you have extra time after completing the activities.

### Did you know?

Interesting facts to extend your background knowledge.

### AQA Examiner's tip

Hints from AQA examiners to help you with your study and to prepare for your exam.

***Commentaries***

Examples of answers you might give to the activities. These are designed to help you to understand what type of response the examiner is looking for. Commentaries sometimes appear directly after the activity and sometimes at the end of the chapter in the section headed Commentaries.

*Summary*

A summary of what is covered in this chapter of the book.

AQA examination questions are reproduced by permission of the Assessment and Qualifications Alliance.

## Web links in the book

As Nelson Thornes is not responsible for third party content online, there may be some changes to this material that are beyond our control. In order for us to ensure that the links referred to in the book are as up-to-date and stable as possible, the websites are usually homepages with supporting instructions on how to reach the relevant pages if necessary.

Please let us know at **kerboodle@nelsonthornes.com** if you find a link that doesn't work and we will do our best to redirect the link, or to find an alternative site.

# Introduction to this book

*Aims of the chapter:*

- explains the content of your A2 English Literature course
- shows how your work for each of the two units of the course will be assessed.

Welcome to A2 English Literature. It is worth reading this first chapter at the start of your course. It will give you some ideas about what is to come, and then you can return to it when you have had more experience of reading your texts and working with this book.

## The course at a glance

A2 English Literature has two units: Unit 3 is taken as a formal exam, Unit 4 is coursework. How the work is divided up in terms of time and teachers will depend very much on the circumstances in the institution you attend – so you could prepare for Unit 3 first and then do Unit 4, or you could prepare for them both simultaneously, or you could do them in reverse numerical order.

It is always worth remembering that across the course as a whole, you will do much more reading and preparation than the examination/coursework can possibly assess. This means that the assessment is a snapshot of what you have been doing rather than the whole process. As we move on to look at how the assessment works, try to see it as a shaping mechanism rather than the be-all and end-all of what A2 English Literature is all about.

## Unit 3: Texts and genres

This unit's title refers to the fact that in this unit your texts will be grouped into two **genres** or generic topics. These are:

- Elements of the Gothic
- Elements of the Pastoral.

### Key terms

**Genre:** a type of text (e.g. a crime novel, a narrative poem). Texts can be grouped and labelled for various reasons, such as their content, their intended audience, how readers respond to them, etc.

Although most students are likely to study one or the other topic, it is possible to answer questions from both sections, although to do this you would need to read more than the minimum number of texts.

In outline, though, you will do the following in preparation for this unit:

- You will read and study at least three texts from a set text list.
- At least one of these texts must come from the sub-section labelled 1300–1800.

You are not allowed to take the texts into the examination with you, which will have significant implications for the way in which you prepare for the examination itself.

The box below outlines the ways in which Unit 3 will be assessed.

### Assessment of Unit 3: Texts and genres

**Exam**: 2 hours
30% of total A Level marks

**Set topics**
Elements of the Gothic
Elements of the Pastoral

**Minimum of three texts for study**, including at least one text 1300–1800

**Two sections, one question to be answered from each section:**

***Section A***

- involves detailed discussion of generic topic as seen in **one** text
- contains specific questions on each of the set texts.

***Section B***

- involves discussing an aspect of the genre across the **three** texts
- contains three questions, wide-ranging in scope.

## Unit 4: Further and independent reading

This is a coursework unit, which, as its title implies, offers the possibility of some independent work. In outline, you will do the following in preparation for this unit:

- read at least two texts with the aim of designing a task that will allow you to compare them
- read and study an anthology of critical material and apply part of it to a text of your choice.

You will produce a portfolio of coursework consisting of two written responses. These are:

- a comparative study of an aspect of two texts
- the application of critical ideas taken from the anthology and applied to a text or texts of your choice.

The box below outlines the ways in which Unit 4 will be assessed.

### Assessment of Unit 4: Further and independent reading

**Coursework**
20% of total A Level marks

**Minimum of three texts for study**, including one pre-released anthology of critical material

**A portfolio of two pieces of written coursework:**
**First piece:** A comparative study of an aspect of two texts. 1500–2000 words
**Second piece:** An application of an aspect of the pre-released critical anthology to a literary text. 1200–1500 words.

## Assessment Objectives

As part of the process by which all specifications are regulated, English Literature is broken down into four Assessment Objectives, or AOs as they are commonly called.

These AOs do not specify the content of your course as such, but they do specify the skills and approaches that you are required to cover. As a student you do not need to worry about covering them, provided you answer the question, either in an examination or for coursework. The question will be designed to cover the skills and approaches – your job is to answer its requirements exactly.

Nonetheless it is useful for you to have an understanding of what these AOs actually say. The box opposite gives them in their official format. But what are their implications in more practical terms?

### AO1

Two key elements combine here: the quality of your writing, and your knowledge of the necessary terminology that goes with this subject. All A Level subjects have their own specialist language and their own academic conventions when it comes to writing. The specialist terminology that you need will emerge as you go through the book, and can be checked in the glossary at the end of the book. It will almost certainly vary among students, depending in particular on which element you choose to study in Unit 3.

**AQA Examiner's tip**

Because the critical anthology counts as one of your core 12 texts in the whole A Level, the text you use to apply to the anthology can be chosen in a number of ways. It could be a new text you have chosen for the purpose, but it could also be a single poem or a text you have studied for a different reason in another part of the course.

**AQA Examiner's tip**

Practise thinking and writing about the significance of **structure** in texts.

***AO1***

Articulate creative, informed and relevant responses to literary texts, using appropriate terminology and concepts, and coherent, accurate written expression.

***AO2***

Demonstrate detailed critical understanding in analysing the ways in which structure, form and language shape meanings in literary texts.

***AO3***

Explore connections and comparisons between different literary texts, informed by interpretations of other readers.

***AO4***

Demonstrate understanding of the significance and influence of the contexts in which literary texts are written and received.

Below are some of the types of writing you could come across during your A2 course:

- Essay in examination, on single text with no copy of the text available.
- Essay in examination, on three texts with no copies of the texts available.
- A coursework essay comparing two texts.
- A further piece of coursework which need not necessarily be in essay format.

Each of these is subtly different, but each needs to be practised and improved. English Literature is all about reading, but it is assessed totally by writing. You therefore need to prepare for your A2 assessments by working at your writing skills, making sure that you know exactly what is required.

## AO2

This is concerned with how texts work and how they are constructed – what authors do with language when they write. The best order in which to take the three key terms is as follows: **form**, **structure**, **language** – that is, the biggest unit first and the smallest last.

Of the three terms, 'language' in a text can often be the easiest to comment on but not necessarily the most useful in terms of developing an argument in an essay.

## AO3

AO3 has two parts to it. It requires that you make connections and comparisons across texts and that when you make these connections you are aware that you are not dealing with absolutes – there are other ways in which the texts can be interpreted, in which case different connections might be made.

At the heart of this idea of interpreting texts through connecting them with others is the idea of **genre**, or type of text. Generic labels help us to identify what a text is like; however, we need to be aware that although it has some qualities in common with the other texts, it may also be different from them. Unit 3 is organised around the idea of genre, and the comparative part of Unit 4 can also lead to work on genre.

In this AO, then, we look for similarity and difference across the texts we are studying, and we will probably find people disagreeing about whether various categories apply. This means that when we are studying Literature we are not dealing with fixed and known interpretations. Part of your work in Unit 3 will involve 'testing' texts against certain generic concepts – and you will probably find that in some ways they follow certain definitions of the genre and in other ways they do not.

## AO4

AO4 follows naturally from AO3, because how you categorise a text depends on various factors, or **contexts**, which shape your response. Contexts can arise from circumstances to do with the way the text was produced, sometimes called *contexts of production*, and contexts to do with the way it is received now, sometimes called *contexts of reception*.

Being aware of the context of a text, and its interpretation, is always important, but you must be careful that you do not allow context to become more important than the text itself. Many of the texts in Unit 3, for example, are 'old' so there can be a strong temptation to start talking in over-general terms about the historical past. While the contexts of production can never be ignored, it is always worth remembering that the text is being read by you in the 21st century because it is still relevant now.

### Key terms

**Form:** the aspects of a text in its totality that enable it to be identified as a novel, or a poem, or an epistolary novel (i.e. a story told in the form of letters), or a sonnet (a poem of 14 lines), etc.

**Structure:** how the significant parts of a text work together to form a whole, e.g. the connection between chapters in a novel, or the way time is organised, or the connection between verses in a poem.

**Language:** in this context, generally refers to specific words or phrases in the text.

**Context:** the circumstances surrounding a text (e.g. where it first appeared, social attitudes today) which affect the way it is understood. The word is formed from *con* (= with) + *text*, so literally it means 'what goes with the text'.

### AQA Examiner's tip

You have heard it stated many times, but the key to doing well in your exam is to answer the question exactly as it is worded. It is the examiners' job to make sure all the technical requirements of the course are met through the questions. It is your job to do exactly as the question states – no more, no less!

*Summary*

This introduction has outlined the content of the A2 course and the way in which it will be assessed, and has raised some issues regarding the course overall. You will find it useful to refer back to it occasionally to keep yourself informed of the overall design of the course.

UNIT 3

# Texts and genres

## Introduction to genre

*Aims of the chapter:*

- introduces Unit 3, Texts and genres
- considers some of the key aspects of the unit.

## What genre is about

- Genres provide a way of classifying and categorising texts. They are a way of deciding what kind of text a particular book is.
- Genre, therefore, creates certain expectations about what we might find in a text, what features will probably be present.
- Genre is not, though, a precise method of identification. The differences between texts within a genre may be as significant as the similarities.

### Breadth

Genres can be very broad, e.g. poetry, or prose, or drama. But the term *genre* can also be used to indicate narrower categories: science fiction or the detective story, for instance. These categories can again be divided into sub-genres: the crime novel, the police procedural, the thriller etc.

### Definitions

The definitions of genre are not precise. For instance, tragedy is often thought of as involving the fall of a great man, frequently also involving huge damage to his native land. However, the American playwright Arthur Miller is often thought of as a tragic dramatist, yet many of the protagonists in his plays are very ordinary people.

### Expectations

You should thus expect to challenge the notion of genre in your readings and ask questions of the genres you explore. Do not expect different writers within a particular genre to see the genre in the same way. Also expect the way any genre is understood to change over time.

## What Unit 3 is about

This unit, which is divided into separate sections on the gothic and the pastoral genres, will:

- introduce you to aspects of the gothic and the pastoral genres
- consider the different ways in which they have been explored by different writers
- compare and contrast some literary texts
- look at some of the contexts of these texts
- give you ideas for your own further study.

# Elements of the Gothic

## 1 The gothic genre

*Aims of the chapter:*

- introduces the gothic genre and some definitions and interpretations of the term 'gothic', in past and present culture
- examines the gothic elements in contrasting texts from different periods.

### What do we mean by 'the Gothic'?

The question is a complex, but important one. The concept of 'the Gothic' has woven itself into our culture, past and present, in many ways and at many levels, and ours is an age in which gothic culture occupies a significant place. The very gothic festival of Hallowe'en is itself worth over £120 million in merchandise sales. Film, fashion and music, as well as much contemporary literature, have all drawn widely on the gothic experience.

#### Activity 1

Make a list of the words or ideas that you associate with the term 'gothic'.

#### *Commentary on Activity 1*

Your first thoughts may well have included references to darkness and monsters of various sorts. Black is an obviously gothic colour, but so, for understandable reasons, is red. You may well have associated particular sorts of setting (both geographical and architectural) with the concept of the Gothic. While it is likely that you have listed ideas about fear, you may also have connected this fear with the oddly pleasurable sensation of being frightened and even the more specifically sexual tension which often characterises gothic narratives.

### Some definitions and other interpretations

#### *From* The Shorter Oxford English Dictionary *(2002)*

1 Of or pertaining to the Goths or their language
2 Designating the style of handwriting used in Western Europe from the 13th century and the typefaces derived from it
3 Designating the style of architecture prevalent in Western Europe from the 12th to the 16th centuries, including such familiar features as the pointed arch and the flying buttress.
4 Belonging to or (supposedly) characteristic of the Middle Ages; medieval, romantic ... redolent of the Dark Ages, portentously gloomy or horrifying
5 Barbarous, crude, uncouth
6 Of or pertaining to the rock music of Goths

Modern Goths

#### *Contemporary Goths*

The Goths referred to in the first definition above were an invading Germanic tribe of the 3rd to the 5th centuries. Those referred to in the last definition are a much more recent phenomenon. One writer has defined the contemporary 'Goth' culture as

> An obsession with all subjects dark and grim ... a view of life that incorporates the world of night as well as the world of day.
>
> ***Nancy Kilpatrick***, The Gothic Bible, *2005*

'Goth' fashions predictably tend to stress black: black trenchcoats, fishnets, and sunglasses. Victorian fashions are also popular: examples include velvet, lace, and long satin dresses. Crosses are a standard accessory.

Goth rock is usually considered to be **introspective**, slow-moving, gloomy, moody and melancholic. Well-known bands include Bauhaus, Joy Division and The Cure.

### *Gothic films*

'Gothic' is a significant genre in film studies, often overlapping with the categories 'horror' and 'thriller'. Important early examples of gothic films include: *The Cabinet of Dr Caligari* (1919); *Frankenstein* (1931); *Dracula* (1931); *Psycho* (1960); the English 'Hammer' films series.

Gothic films tend to follow certain conventions:

- Much of the action takes place at night.
- Women are typically represented as victims.
- There is a set of familiar physical settings and other visual elements (dark skies, ruined buildings, shadows, staring eyes).
- The aim is to induce fear in the audience (but also, **ironically**, a comforting sense of the safety of perspective).
- The central male **protagonist** is often defined by his actions rather than by complex personality attributes; his role is to defeat 'the monster'.
- The plot often involves a journey, a pursuit and a rescue.

### *Other aspects of 'gothic'*

- **A fascination with the past, especially the medieval past**: You may also have noticed that forms of the gothic style occur during different historical periods. What historians call the 'Gothic Revival', for instance, was an important influence on the architecture of Victorian England.
- **Overtones of the savage or barbarous**: Literary critics have often been dismissive of what they saw as simply **sensational** literature. Dr Johnson referred to what he called 'this wild strain of imagination' and Samuel Taylor Coleridge made this comment on Matthew Lewis's *The Monk*: 'with how little expense of thought or imagination this species of composition is manufactured.'
- **The tendency to employ symbolism of light and darkness**: These effects can be used both literally and **metaphorically**.
- **Psychological connotations**: many gothic characters are brooding, disturbed beings. This idea will be further explored at a later stage, as will many of the others listed above.

#### Key terms

**Introspective:** inward-looking, self-examining.

**Irony:** a broad term which has many different applications. Essentially irony creates effects by meaning the opposite of what it says. Inevitably, therefore, readers have to be alert to this, or they fail to get the 'real' point.

**Protagonist:** the principal character in a narrative, often but not always the hero or heroine.

**Sensational:** designed merely to appeal to the emotions.

**Metaphorically:** not literally; an implied comparison as if the subject were something that it merely resembles.

**Connotations:** the implications and associations of a word (rather than the directly represented meaning).

#### Did you know?

Hitchcock famously sent out an order to all cinemas playing *Psycho*, saying that the manager of the cinema had been instructed 'at the risk of his life, not to admit any persons after the picture starts'. In this, and several other ways, Hitchcock took great pains to manipulate the audience experience of watching the film.

## Contemporary gothic culture

Contemporary interest in gothic culture takes many forms. There are spoof television series such as *The Munsters* and *The Addams Family* (also available in two film adaptations, based on the original cartoons by Charles Addams), and long-running dramas such as *Buffy the Vampire Slayer* and *The X-Files*. *Young Dracula* is a popular children's television

**AQA Examiner's tip**

In the examination you will be asked to show that you understand that texts can be interpreted in different ways. Build this understanding into your studies from the start.

**Link**

For a commentary on Activity 2, see the end of the chapter.

programme. *Edward Scissorhands* and *Sleepy Hollow* are two popular films with a gothic theme. There are many gothic websites and a huge range of computer games with gothic elements. Popular gothic magazines include *Ascension Magazine*, *Comatose Rose*, and *Elegy*.

### Activity 2

Read the following article, taken from *Bite Me Magazine*, and list its gothic features. Are there any aspects of the text that mark it as 21st-century Gothic?

> **Sweeney Todd is new dungeon 'hair-raiser'**
>
> Demon barber Sweeney Todd is to join the villainous cast at the capital's scariest attraction at London Dungeon. The new 'cut throat' experience was recently unveiled and marks the Dungeon's first departure from the strictly historical. 'The Sweeney Todd story has been recounted so many times in books, on stage and on film that most people believe he was a real character. The blurring of myth with reality has been so profound we felt Sweeney Todd was now deserving of a Dungeon starring role, alongside the likes of Jack the Ripper and dark events like the Great Plague,' said Dungeon boss Colin Thomas.
>
> Thought to have made their first appearance in a Penny Dreadful – cheap thrillers of the late 19th century – Sweeney Todd and his pie-making partner-in-crime Mrs Lovett were featured in a recent gritty BBC (version), with Ray Winstone in the title role. 'There are even well-advanced plans for a new Hollywood version of the story,' said Colin. The dungeon's telling of the tale is likely to be more terrifying than either ... beginning in a dark and smoggy 18th-century Fleet Street where visitors will be greeted by Mrs Lovett and urged to take their seats for a trim. They will then be plunged into total darkness and visited by the disembodied voice of Sweeney himself.

Bite Me Magazine, *Issue 19 (2007), p7*

Reference to earlier versions of the story emphasises the longevity of the gothic genre, and its adaptability. You will be considering the different forms and periods of the Gothic at a later stage in this chapter.

**Did you know?**

Edgar Allan Poe's early death at the age of 40 has been ascribed to causes as various as epilepsy and alcoholism. Film adaptations of such of his tales as *The Masque of the Red Death*, *The Pit and the Pendulum* and *The Fall of the House of Usher* have proved hugely popular examples of the gothic genre.

## American gothic

Edgar Allan Poe's *The Raven* (1845) is a famous example of American gothic.

### Activity 3

Read the opening three verses below. In what ways do you think this poem might be considered 'gothic'?

You might begin with these questions:

1. What typical gothic motifs (dominant ideas or images) are used?
2. Look for these additional elements: the position of the narrator; the appeal to the senses; the creation of tension. How do these operate?
3. How does the poetic form influence the gothic effect?

Once upon a midnight dreary, while I pondered, weak and weary
Over many a quaint and curious volume of forgotten lore –
While I nodded, nearly napping, suddenly there came a tapping,
As of someone gently rapping, rapping at my chamber door,
''Tis some visitor,' I muttered, 'tapping at my chamber door –
Only this and nothing more.'

Ah, distinctly I remember it was in the bleak December;
And each separate dying ember wrought its ghost upon the floor.
Eagerly I wished the morrow; vainly I had sought to borrow
From my books surcease of sorrow – sorrow for the lost Lenore –
For the rare and radiant maiden whom the angels name Lenore –
Nameless here for evermore.

And the silken, sad uncertain rustling of each purple curtain
Thrilled me – filled me with fantastic terrors never felt before:
So that now, to still the beating of my heart, I stood repeating,
''Tis some visitor entreating entrance at my chamber door –
Some late visitor entreating entrance at my chamber door –
This it is and nothing more.'

***Edgar Allan Poe** from* The Raven, *1845*

### Link

For a commentary on Activity 3, see the end of the chapter.

### Extension activities

1. Read the rest of the poem (using the extract link) and explore its narrative structure.
2. Study some other works by Edgar Allan Poe. Possible choices include *The Masque of the Red Death*, *The Fall of the House of Usher*, *The Pit and the Pendulum*, *The Cask of Amontillado*.
3. Poe was an American writer. Have you found gothic elements in any other American literature that you have read? (Tennessee Williams is a possible choice here, for instance.)

## What elements of the Gothic have been identified so far?

So far we have identified the following features:

- a fondness for the symbols of darkness and light
- a significant use of the setting
- the creation of fear as a narrative priority
- a focus on the influence of the past
- a difference between male and female roles which themselves often follow particular conventions
- a blurring of reality and fantasy, being awake and dreaming, within the tales
- a tendency for certain psychological traits to occur within the main characters.

## Commentaries

### *Commentary on Activity 2*

There is interesting reference made here to the 'blurring of **myth** with reality' that you may find characteristic of the way the Gothic mixes fable and fact. The phrase 'scariest attraction' **foregrounds** the idea that fear can be induced with pleasurable effects. The word 'story' reflects the importance of narrative within the gothic genre, and in your analysis of narrative methods you should be able to draw on skills learned during the AS course.

There are familiar elements such as 'dungeon', 'dark' and 'villainous' here, but you also may have noticed more modern **blends** such as 'smoggy' and the word play involved in '"cut throat" experience' and 'pie-making partner-in-crime' that suggest the register of popular journalism.

### *Commentary on Activity 3*

You will probably have noticed the position adopted by the first-person narrator, and may have ascribed certain qualities to the narrative voice: anguished, brooding, lonely, uncertain, introspective. The situational context appears to be that of a drifting between awake and sleep; the world of dreams seems close at hand. The narrative begins 'at midnight'. There is some characteristic gothic vocabulary and **imagery**: 'midnight dreary', 'bleak December', 'dying ember', 'ghost', 'sorrow', 'lost'.

Interest in the past is **signified** by the traditional words 'once upon', here followed by a specified time. The book the narrator is reading is a 'quaint' volume of 'forgotten lore'; there is a sense of regret for the loss of a half-remembered past.

The woman is described in significant terms; she is presented as a rather **ethereal** figure: 'rare and radiant' and associated with angels, but now 'nameless'. Perception comes to the narrator largely through hearing, but the sounds are indistinct and resist certain interpretation. Tension is created and built up through 'the beating of my heart'.

You may also have noticed the hypnotic, incantatory rhyme and rhythm, the very distinctive poetic form with its repetitions and internal rhymes, and the **refrain** of the last line with its emphatic and perhaps delusional negatives. These all contribute to the gothic effect through their insistent, remorseless patterns, and the eerie, rather dream-like mood they create.

*Summary*

In this introductory chapter you have looked at a range of definitions and interpretations of The Gothic, including gothic films and contemporary gothic culture. You have identified some key elements of The Gothic and studied the gothic elements in two contrasting texts from different periods.

### Key terms

**Myth:** a complex term, usually referring to a story that is not 'true' and deals with the supernatural and ideas of creation.

**Foreground:** in a piece of writing, to draw attention to something by means of a particular expression or use of language.

**Blend:** a word formulation where two words are blended together – in this case 'smoke' and 'fog' – to form a new one (smog).

**Images/imagery:** the representation of ideas, objects and states of mind through an associated network of references.

**Signify:** to convey meaning through a 'sign', here a linguistic feature, the phrase that conveys particular meanings and associations.

**Ethereal:** heavenly, unearthly.

**Refrain:** a phrase or lines repeated at intervals during a poem.

### Remember

**Introspective** was defined earlier in this chapter.

### AQA Examiner's tip

Always ensure that you look closely at how a writer uses language. Try to consider how their use of language shapes the meanings of the text.

# 2 Place and setting in the Gothic

*Aims of the chapter:*

- considers aspects of settings (both buildings and landscape) that are typical of gothic literature
- studies and compares the gothic elements in a range of texts describing place and setting, and considers the part they play in the narrative.

## Key terms

**Topography:** natural and man-made features of a geographical area.

**Vertiginous:** tending to induce dizziness.

**Neo-classicism:** style in architecture and art (especially from the mid-18th to early 19th century) inspired by the models of classical Greece and Rome. 'Neo' is from the Greek word *neos*, meaning 'new'.

## Did you know?

There is more than one gothic period in the history of English architecture. What is sometimes called the Early Gothic style developed in the 12th century, examples of which can be seen in York Minster and Hexham Abbey in the north of England. A gothic revival occurred in the 19th century, often divided into the Early Victorian and Late Victorian periods. The Palace of Westminster, built during these years, has become a famous national symbol.

## Gothic fiction: place and setting

### Activity 1

Consider these settings. Which seem to you to have gothic potential, and for what reasons?

An abbey; a ruined castle; a railway station; a crypt; a forest; a country house; a graveyard; a spaceship; an office block; a theatre; a factory; a prison (does 'dungeon' suggest something different?); an island; a school or college

***Commentary on Activity 1***

Your previous studies will have taught you the significance of place within narrative. Gothic fiction has a characteristic **topography**, and place and setting operate within the gothic narrative in particular ways.

Gothic architecture, such as cathedrals and abbeys, was characterised by pointed arches and flying buttresses, stained-glass windows, and rib vaults. The effect on the spectator was often frightening and **vertiginous**. Also associated with gothic architecture were gargoyles, which are grotesque carvings of men and animals protruding from roofs and walls.

Gothic literary landscapes are often equally wild and exotic, a wilderness in which extreme actions and passions seem oddly appropriate to the setting. Remember, also, from the perspective of 18th-century **neo-classicism**, Gothic was synonymous with what was crude and barbaric. The settings often play a significant part in the unfolding of the narrative: their features may directly influence the action; they may also symbolise some aspects of the personalities of the protagonists.

In your consideration of the settings listed in the activity you may have felt that the abbey, castle, crypt and graveyard were clearly 'gothic' settings, and the theatre, factory and railway station were less so. But consider the very gothic qualities of *The Phantom of the Opera*, set in and around the Paris Opera House. The Midland Grand Hotel at St Pancras Station, in London, is one of the most famous examples of Victorian Gothic architecture in Britain. It is possible that a very wide range of settings might be incorporated into the gothic world, depending on how they are used.

*Gothic architecture*

## Link

For a commentary on Activity 2, see the end of the chapter.

## Did you know?

*The Castle of Otranto* (1764) is often thought of as the first gothic novel. It contains almost all of the traditional features of the gothic tale, from ominous ghosts to fearful women trapped in underground labyrinths.

## Language hint

**Contiguous:** next to, adjoining

**Cloisters:** an enclosed space, possibly a courtyard, within a monastery or nunnery

## Activity 2

Read the following passage from Horace Walpole's *The Castle of Otranto* (1764) and consider which aspects of its setting might be considered 'gothic'. The extract comes from the first chapter of the novel. The innocent Isabella is in flight from Manfred and his incestuous desires.

> Yet where conceal herself! How avoid the pursuit he would infallibly make throughout the castle! As these thoughts passed rapidly through her mind, she recollected a subterraneous passage which led from the vaults of the castle to the church of Saint Nicholas. Could she reach the altar before she was overtaken, she knew even Manfred's violence would not dare to profane the sacredness of the place; and she determined, if no other means of deliverance offered, to shut herself up for ever among the holy virgins, whose convent was contiguous to the cathedral. In this resolution, she seized a lamp that burned at the foot of the staircase, and hurried towards the secret passage.
>
> The lower part of the castle was hollowed into several intricate cloisters; and it was not easy for one under so much anxiety to find the door that opened into the cavern. An awful silence reigned throughout those subterraneous regions, except now and then some blasts of wind that shook the doors she had passed, and which grating on the rusty hinges were re-echoed through that long labyrinth of darkness.

***Horace Walpole***, The Castle of Otranto, *p61*

Still focusing on the landscape of Gothic, here are two passages from different works by the same author, Robert Louis Stevenson, whose novel *Dr Jekyll and Mr Hyde* (1886) is often considered to be a classic example of the gothic genre.

The first extract is from his autobiographical *Travels with a Donkey in the Cévennes* (1879). Stevenson, at this stage of his journey, has lost his way and is seeking a place to camp for the night.

> At last black trees began to show upon my left, and, suddenly crossing the road, made a cave of unmitigated blackness right in front. I call it a cave without exaggeration; to pass below that arch of leaves was like entering a dungeon. I felt about until my hand encountered a stout branch, and to this I tied Modestine, a haggard, drenched, desponding donkey. Then I lowered my pack, laid it along the wall on the margin of the road, and un-buckled the straps. I knew well enough where the lantern was: but where were the candles? I groped and groped among the tumbled articles, and, while I was thus groping, suddenly I touched the spirit-lamp. Salvation! This would serve my turn as well. The wind roared unwearyingly among the trees; I could hear the boughs tossing and the leaves churning through half a mile of forest; yet the scene of my encampment was not only as black as the pit, but admirably sheltered. At the second match the wick caught flame. The light was both livid and shifting; but it cut me off from the universe, and doubled the darkness of the surrounding night.

***R.L. Stevenson***, Travels with a Donkey in the Cévennes, *p46*

The second extract is from Stevenson's historical novel *Kidnapped* (1886). David Balfour has been sent by his treacherous uncle to climb the broken stair-tower.

> The house of Shaws stood some five full storeys high, not counting lofts. Well, as I advanced, it seemed to me the stair grew airier and a thought more lightsome; and I was wondering what might be the cause of this change, when a second blink of the summer lightning came and went. If I did not cry out, it was because fear had me by the throat; and if I did not fall, it was more by heaven's mercy than my own strength. It was not only that the flash shone in on every side through breaches in the wall, so that I seemed to be clambering aloft upon an open scaffold, but the same passing brightness showed me that the steps were of unequal length, and that one of my feet rested that moment within two inches of the well …
>
> The darkness, by contrast with the flash, appeared to have redoubled; nor was that all, for my ears were now troubled and my mind confounded by a great stir of bats in the top part of the tower, and the foul beasts, flying downward, sometimes beat about my face and body.

***R.L. Stevenson***, Kidnapped, *p22*

## Activity 3

What are the significant similarities and differences in the way the gothic elements operate in these two texts? Is it important that the second text is what is normally thought of as 'fiction', the first 'non-fiction'?

### Link

For a commentary on Activity 3, see the end of the chapter.

## Activity 4

Now look at two more extracts. Both of these are set in a polar region, not usually considered a 'gothic' environment. Are there features of these settings, or in their representation, that might be thought of as gothic?

### AQA Examiner's tip

Learning how to compare and contrast texts will be an important part of your course. You need to decide which are the most significant areas for comparison and which are less important. In the extracts above, the different ways in which Stevenson works within the gothic genre form the main focus of the analysis.

### Link

For a commentary on Activity 4, see the end of the chapter.

The first extract is from *Scott's Last Expedition*, the journals of Captain Scott on his journey to the South Pole in 1912.

> Wednesday, January 17. – Camp 69. T. –22 at start. Night –21. The pole. Yes, but under very different circumstances from those expected. We have had a horrible day – add to our disappointment a head wind 4 to 5, with a temperature –22, and companions labouring on with cold feet and hands.
>
> We started at 7.30, none of us having slept much after the shock of our discovery [that the Norwegians had reached the pole first].
>
> … To-night little Bowers is laying himself out to get sights in terrible difficult circumstances; the wind is blowing hard. T. –21, and there is that curious damp cold feeling in the air which chills one to the bone in no time. We have been descending again, I think, but there looks to be a rise ahead; otherwise there is very little that is different from the awful monotony of past days. Great God! This is an awful place and terrible enough for us to have laboured to it without the reward of priority. Well, it is something to have got here, and the wind may be our friend tomorrow.

***Captain R.F. Scott***, Scott's Last Expedition, *p424*

The second extract is from the last chapter of Mary Shelley's *Frankenstein*, in which Frankenstein, on the trail of the monster, has reached the Arctic, and found that the monster has fled across the ice.

> On hearing this information I suffered a temporary access of despair. He had escaped me, and I must commence a destructive and almost endless journey across the mountainous ices of the ocean, amidst cold that few of the inhabitants could long endure, and which I, the native of a genial and sunny climate, could not hope to survive. Yet at the idea that the fiend should live and be triumphant, my rage and vengeance returned, and like a mighty tide, overwhelmed every other feeling. After a slight repose, during which the spirits of the dead hovered around and instigated me to toil and revenge, I prepared for my journey.
>
> I exchanged my land-sledge for one fashioned for the inequalities of the frozen ocean, and purchasing a plentiful stock of provisions, I departed from land.
>
> I cannot guess how many days have passed since then, but I have endured misery which nothing but the eternal sentiment of a just retribution burning within my heart could have enabled me to support. Immense and rugged mountains of ice often barred up my passage, and I often heard the thunder of the ground sea, which threatened my destruction. But again the frost came and made the paths of the sea secure.

***Mary Shelley***, Frankenstein, *p200*

## Extension activity

Explore the settings of a range of gothic texts and compare and contrast the ways in which writers create a gothic effect from very different environments.

Possible examples include:

- Hell in Books 1 and 2 of John Milton's *Paradise Lost*
- The coastal castle of Angela Carter's 'The Bloody Chamber'
- Bram Stoker's Transylvania in *Dracula*
- The house known as 'Wuthering Heights', in Emily Brontë's novel of the same name
- The laboratory in Mary Shelley's *Frankenstein*
- Macbeth's castle.

## Commentaries

### *Commentary on Activity 2*

Here are some possible ideas:

1 There are the familiar elements of a chase and pursuit, closely linked to the internal design of the castle.

2 Several words and phrases convey a sense of darkness and the underground: 'subterraneous' (repeated), 'vaults', 'foot of the staircase', 'lower part of the castle', 'cavern'. All of these convey a sense both of physical depth and the emotional depth of despair.

3 The religious associations of such words as 'church', 'altar', 'cathedral', 'convent' provide a moral opposition to the sense of darkness and evil.

4 Mystery and a sense of suspense are conveyed by such references as 'secret passage'.
5 The idea of imprisonment is foreshadowed by Isabella's resolution to 'shut herself up'.
6 The sense of being lost within the building is repeatedly emphasised: 'labyrinth', 'intricate'. Note how the **syntax** is often equally elaborated.
7 The experience of being trapped within the building is conveyed through references to sound: 'silence reigned', 'blasts of wind', 'grating', 're-echoed'.
8 In general, physical features of place and setting act as a means of conveying and representing the feelings and personalities of the characters.

### Key terms

**Syntax:** the study of the relationship between words and other units within a sentence.

## *Commentary on Activity 3*

### Travels with a Donkey

Here Stevenson is exploring both his own emotions and the nature of the landscape in which he finds himself. Words such as 'black', 'blackness', 'cave' and 'dungeon' convey the familiar gothic elements of fear and imprisonment. The narrative is first person, and experience is conveyed through close references to the senses, especially hearing and touch – appropriately enough, considering the darkness that surrounds him. The contrast between light and darkness is stressed: lantern, spirit-lamp and wick come from human agency; the darkness is elemental. Religious terminology is used to convey this sense of threat and rescue: 'salvation' and 'black as the pit'.

You may feel, however, that the tone is distinctively different here from that of the second text. There's a sort of self-parody and sense of the ridiculous in the author's depiction of his predicament, despite the strong sense of final isolation. After all, the donkey is probably suffering more than Stevenson.

You may have decided that the distinction between fictional and non-fictional texts is not very useful here. Does it make a great difference to your reading to know that the events described in the first extract actually happened to Stevenson? Can we, anyway, ever be sure that autobiographical accounts are wholly 'true'? Both extracts involve similar narrative features and explore some similar emotional reactions to their setting. Your methods of analysis of the two texts ultimately may not have been very different.

### Kidnapped

You can probably find several architectural features characteristic of gothic literature here. There is reference to unnerving height, broken stairs, towers etc. Imagery such as 'scaffold' helps to establish the sense of threat and mortality. The dramatic effect of the weather is stressed, but it also brings in references to supernatural powers, in this case salutary.

The intrusion of the bats adds a familiar gothic element; here they also reflect a range of conflicting sensations within the narrator. In general, this passage lacks any of the sense of distance of the first; the narrator seems to be more helpless in the face of the physical threat offered by his environment.

### *Commentary on Activity 4*

One feature you may have noticed is the relationship of the protagonists to their surroundings; to an extent they are defined by their response to the setting. Both protagonists are driven men and both respond emotionally to the awesome and hostile terrain: 'disappointment', 'shock', 'despair', 'misery', etc. In both cases, also, the setting is directly linked to the extreme nature of their suffering and endurance. Humanity is in some ways dwarfed by the immensity of the polar ice mountains, but you may also feel that the narrators gain heroic stature from their struggle. The very gothic threat of death is always present here, but so is a sense of the sublime. The soaring heights and dizzying perspectives of medieval cathedrals and ruined castles are replicated in the walls of ice and snow that confront our travellers.

*Summary*

In this chapter you have looked at some of the typical settings to be found in gothic literature, from gothic architecture to wild landscapes. You have studied and compared texts in which setting is an important feature of the narrative, and have learnt that settings may influence the action, represent the feelings and personalities of the characters and help to convey central themes of the texts.

# 3 The gothic protagonist

*Aims of the chapter:*

- considers some of the characteristic features of gothic protagonists as depicted in a range of texts from different periods
- looks at the different ways in which readers might respond to these characters.

### Remember

**Protagonist** was defined in Chapter 1.

### Key terms

**Epic:** a long narrative – often a poem – on a heroic scale, dealing with great deeds, dangerous journeys and outsize characters. Tolkien's *The Lord of the Rings* is one example of an epic.

### Did you know?

John Milton was a significant figure in Oliver Cromwell's Commonwealth during the 1640s and 1650s. By 1652, however, he was completely blind, and *Paradise Lost* was written by dictation.

### Language hint

**Baleful:** hostile and destructive

**Obdurate:** stubborn

### Did you know?

Although Milton set out in *Paradise Lost* to 'justify the ways of God to man', some critics have argued that Satan is the most dynamic and heroic figure in the poem. The Romantic poet and artist William Blake felt that Milton 'was of the Devil's party without knowing it'.

### Activity 1

Create your own gothic protagonist. Write a brief description of someone that you could imagine as being the main character in a gothic tale. Include reference to physical appearance. Compare and contrast your creations with those of others in your group.

***Commentary on Activity 1***

It is likely, of course, that there will be many important differences between your creations, but there may also be interesting common features. For instance, you may have looked at aspects of age, gender, voice, dominant colouring (hair, clothes etc.) and possibly significant setting. Is the profession or nationality of any of the characters identified? Are they engaged in significant activity?

The status of the character may have been significant. However powerful they are, there is often a feeling that gothic protagonists are in some way flawed; there is often a sense of impending doom hanging over them.

Now look at a famous example of a doomed gothic protagonist.

## Milton's Satan as a gothic protagonist

Critics have often commented on the ways in which John Milton's Satan has provided a model for the doomed central characters of gothic novels. In Book 1 of his **epic** poem *Paradise Lost* (1667), Milton describes the fall of Satan and his fellow rebel angels, cast out by God from Heaven into the terrible darkness of Hell.

In this extract, Satan reflects on his terrible fall. What he sees around him fills him with despair.

> now the thought
> Both of lost happiness and lasting pain
> Torments him: round he throws his baleful eyes,
> That witnessed huge affliction and dismay
> Mixed with obdurate pride and steadfast hate.
>
> At once, as far as Angels ken, he views
> The dismal situation waste and wild.
> A dungeon horrible, on all sides round,
> As one great furnace flamed; yet from those flames
> No light; but rather darkness visible …

Paradise Lost, *Book 1, lines 54–63*

Here Milton stresses the degree to which, however defiantly he acts, Satan is subject to God's power.

> So stretched out huge in length the Arch-fiend lay,
> Chained on the burning lake; nor ever thence
> Had risen, or heaved his head, but that the will
> And high permission of all-ruling heaven
> Left him at large to his own dark designs,

### Language hint

**Reiterated:** repeated

**Seduced:** tempted

That with reiterated crimes he might
Heap on himself damnation, while he sought
Evil to others, and enraged might see
How all his malice served but to bring forth
Infinite goodness, grace and mercy, shewn
On man by him seduced, but on himself
Treble confusion, wrath and vengeance poured.

Paradise Lost, *Book 1, lines 209–20*

### Link

For a commentary on Activity 2, see the end of the chapter.

### Activity 2

Discuss which aspects of Milton's Satan remind you of the central protagonists in any gothic novels you have read.

## Other gothic protagonists

The following descriptions of central characters are taken from two gothic novels written almost 170 years apart: *The Woman in Black* by Susan Hill (1983) and *Frankenstein* by Mary Shelley (1818).

In the first two extracts from *The Woman in Black*, the narrator, Arthur Kipps, is forced to recall past events. In the third extract he describes the feelings that overcame him in Eel Marsh House.

*An illustration by Gustave Doré of Satan for* Paradise Lost

> I was then thirty-five and I had been a widower for the past twelve years. I had no taste at all for social life and, although in good general health, was prone to occasional nervous illnesses and conditions, as a result of the experiences I will come to relate. Truth to tell, I was growing old before my time, a sombre, pale-complexioned man with a strained expression – a dull dog. …
>
> I had never been an imaginative or fanciful man and certainly not one given to visions of the future. Indeed, since those earlier experiences I had deliberately avoided all contemplation of any remotely non-material matters, and clung to the prosaic, the visible and the tangible. …
>
> I was still a young man. Apart from the inevitable loss of elderly aunts and uncles and grandparents I had never experienced the death of anyone close to me, never truly mourned and suffered the extremes of grief. Never yet. But the feelings that must accompany the death of someone as close to my heart and bound up with my own being as it was possible to be, I knew then, in the nursery of Eel Marsh House. They all but broke me, yet I was confused and puzzled, not knowing any reason at all why I should be in the grip of such desperate anguish and misery. It was as though I had, for the time that I was in the room, become another person, or at least experienced the emotions that belong to another.

***Susan Hill,*** The Woman in Black, *pp11, 13, 127–8*

### AQA Examiner's tip

Develop a glossary of critical vocabulary that will allow you to comment precisely on writers' techniques. Don't merely identify features of style, but try to explain how they help to convey the meanings of the text.

In this extract from *Frankenstein*, Victor Frankenstein recounts a pivotal moment in his youth.

> Such were the professor's words – rather let me say such the words of the fate – enounced to destroy me. As he went on I felt as if my soul were grappling with a palpable enemy; one by one the various keys were touched which formed the mechanism of my being:

> chord after chord was sounded, and soon my mind was filled with one thought, one conception, one purpose. So much has been done, exclaimed the soul of Frankenstein, – more, far more will I achieve: treading in the steps already marked, I will pioneer a new way, explore unknown powers, and unfold to the world the deepest mysteries of creation.

***Mary Shelley***, Frankenstein, *p47*

### Did you know?

Mary Shelley was at the centre of one of the most important literary groups of the 19th century. She was the daughter of William Godwin and Mary Wollstonecraft, both famous radical thinkers and writers of the time. She was a friend of Lord Byron and married Percy Shelley, one of the most celebrated and controversial of the Romantic poets.

### Activity 3

1. What sort of narrative voices do we have in the above extracts?
2. In what ways is the past significant to these characters?
3. Are there other significant similarities and differences between the two narrators?

### Link

For a commentary on Activity 3, see the end of the chapter.

## The gothic protagonist and sexuality

These two selections are from works written nearly 200 years apart: Angela Carter's short story 'The Bloody Chamber' (1979) and Matthew Lewis's novel *The Monk* (1796). Here the gothic protagonist is presented with a much more significant emphasis on their sexuality.

The narrator in 'The Bloody Chamber' first confronts her emotions before her wedding night and in the second extract struggles to convey her sense of her husband's emotions even after she has discovered the horror of his intentions.

> And I began to shudder, like a race horse before a race, yet also with a kind of fear, for I felt both a strange, impersonal arousal at the thought of love and at the same time a repugnance I could not stifle for his white, heavy flesh that had too much in common with the armfuls of arum lilies that filled my bedroom in great glass jars, those undertakers' lilies that powder your fingers as if you had dipped them in turmeric. The lilies I always associate with him; that are white. And stain you. …
>
> And it seemed to me he was in despair.
>
> Strange. In spite of my fear of him, that made me whiter than my wrap, I felt there emanate from him, at that moment, a stench of absolute despair, rank and ghastly, as if the lilies that surrounded him had all at once began to fester, or the Russian leather of his scent were reverting to the elements of flayed hide and excrement of which it was composed. The chthonic gravity of his presence exerted a tremendous pressure on the room, so that the blood pounded in my ears as if we had been precipitated to the bottom of the sea, beneath the waves that pounded against the shore.

***Angela Carter****, 'The Bloody Chamber', pp15, 35*

Here are two descriptions of Ambrosio, the monk of the title of Matthew Lewis's novel. The first is provided by Don Christoval, a Spanish nobleman, and represents the adulation in which the monk was held by the people of Madrid. In the second the narrator sums up the effect of the church's teaching on Ambrosio's early life.

### Did you know?

In his early years Matthew Lewis worked as an attaché to the British Embassy in The Hague (and later sat in the House of Commons). At the age of 19 he created a sensation with his novel *The Monk* and as 'Monk' Lewis found himself invited into fashionable society where he met Byron and Sir Walter Scott.

> The late Superior of the capuchins found him while yet an Infant at the Abbey-door. All attempts to discover who had left him there were vain, and the Child himself could give no account of his Parents … In the whole course of his life He has never been known to transgress a single rule of his order; The smallest stain is not to be discovered upon his character; and He is reported to be so strict an observer of Chastity, that He knows not in what consists the difference of man and Woman. The common People therefore esteem him to be a Saint …
>
> His instructors carefully repressed those virtues, whose grandeur and disinterestedness were ill-suited to the Cloister. Instead of universal benevolence He adopted a selfish partiality for his own particular establishment: He was taught to consider compassion for the errors of Others as a crime of the blackest dye: The noble frankness of his temper was exchanged for servile humility; and in order to break his natural spirit, the Monks terrified his young mind, by placing before him all the horrors with which Superstition could furnish them: they painted to him the torments of the Damned in colours of the most dark, terrible, and fantastic, and threatened him at the slightest fault with eternal perdition … While the Monks were busied in rooting out his virtues, and narrowing his sentiments, they allowed every vice which had fallen to his share, to arrive at full perfection. He was suffered to be proud, vain, ambitious and disdainful: he was jealous of his Equals, and despised all merit but his own: He was implacable when offended, and cruel in his revenge.

***Matthew Lewis***, The Monk, *pp16–17, 237*

## Link

For a commentary on Activity 4, see the end of the chapter.

## Activity 4

Consider in relation to the central protagonists in the above extracts:

1. the sexual elements in the narratives
2. the effect of the exotic setting
3. any other significantly similar or different narrative features.

## Extension activity

Explore the central features of the gothic protagonists in any of these works:

- The Old Man in *The Pardoner's Tale* by Geoffrey Chaucer (c.1395)
- *Dr Faustus* by Christopher Marlowe (1604)
- *Frankenstein* by Mary Shelley (1818)
- *The Fall of the House of Usher* by Edgar Allan Poe (1840)
- *Wuthering Heights* by Emily Brontë (1847)
- *Dracula* by Bram Stoker (1897)
- *The Gormenghast Trilogy* by Mervyn Peake (1946)

Consider whether in these texts a gothic protagonist is balanced against another, more passive, character within the narrative. Alternatively, do you find that the second character plays a more active, even heroic, role?

## Characteristic features of the gothic protagonist summarised

So far we have identified several features of the gothic protagonist:

- some degree of tragic stature
- of high social rank
- somehow foreshadowed by doom
- a tendency to be influenced by past events
- sharply contrasting qualities within the character
- the possession of considerable powers
- a striking physical presence
- a strongly sexual element
- driven by some all-consuming passion
- a connection with the exotic
- an occasional association with what is bestial or non-human.

# Commentaries

### *Commentary on Activity 2*

Satan is both defiant and doomed. His stature is acknowledged here, not only in his physical immensity, 'huge in length', but also by association with the environment in which he is placed, 'The dismal situation waste and wild'. There is also, however, a clear sense that Satan is not in control of his own fate; more powerful forces will shape his destiny.

Satan is also trapped and tormented by the past and the likely future, 'the thought / Both of lost happiness and lasting pain'. In desperation, his only consolation seems to be the thought of further pain that he can cause others ('he sought evil to others'), but his eventual doom seems assured. **Images** of light and darkness dominate the scene. These represent both the physical environment and aspects of Satan's own character. This sense of sharp contrasts, of **binary opposites**, may be significant in the ways that you respond to the central characters in gothic fiction.

Another interesting aspect of Milton's presentation of Satan lies in the character's relationship with the supernatural. In this respect and in others Satan has many of the characteristics of the tragic hero: a figure of huge powers and potential, but thwarted by the destructive elements within their character.

#### Key terms

**Images:** the representation of ideas, objects and states of mind through an associated network of references.

**Binary opposites:** a linguistic term for firmly or conventionally associated contrasting pairs in which the relationship between the two concepts is central to the understanding of both.

### *Commentary on Activity 3*

You will have noticed that both texts have first-person narrators, and narrators who clearly play a significant part in the plot. Arthur Kipps, perhaps characteristically of gothic novels, is a white middle-class male. He is also a solicitor, and is at pains to establish his credentials as a narrator by denying that he is given to flights of fancy or excessive use of the imagination. Thus we are encouraged to see him as stable and rational (perhaps qualities that we associate with his profession), and also to presume that matters which are *not* 'prosaic, visible and tangible' will come to dominate the story.

Despite his rather plain, unaffected style, a sense of underlying strain is conveyed, and in the last extract there is repeated reference to strong emotions: 'confused and puzzled', 'anguish and misery'. The effect of the complex and periodic syntactical structures is to throw emphasis on key words: 'Eel Marsh House', 'misery' and 'another'; a sense of his transformation is finally stressed.

The references to time (note the repeated word 'never' and his stress on the comparatively untroubled nature of his early years) suggest the significance of the past to him.

Frankenstein comes from a similar social group, but is a scientist and something of a philosopher rather than a solicitor. His narrative voice is more obviously **rhetorical** and literary: note the extended musical **metaphor** and the later use of the language of travel and exploration. We may expect this narrator to play a more active, even heroic, role within the tale. He also, however, clearly sees himself as a victim of the past, as his bitter reflections show.

### Key terms

**Rhetorical:** using rhetoric – the art of persuasion.

**Metaphor:** an umbrella term for sub-branches such as **simile**, metaphor involves the comparison of one thing, action, etc. with another. When seen in longer stretches of text, with different metaphors taken from the same area of meaning, this is often called **imagery**.

## *Commentary on Activity 4*

### 'The Bloody Chamber'

The narrator in 'The Bloody Chamber' is female, and this has a significant effect on the depiction of the mixture of fear and desire that dominates the first extract. Again the narrator is placed as a largely passive victim, but the threat, if that is what it is, is more overtly sexual. The context of the approaching wedding night is, of course, important here, and carries with it many social implications. The flowers carry a range of associations, and the colour white is unusually used to convey unease.

The slightly exotic impact of the sense-driven narrative is developed in the second extract. Here the strangeness of the male protagonist is emphasised again through strongly sensual elements and in one instance specifically linked to 'the Russian leather of his scent'. The word 'chthonic' evokes the underworld, and such narratives as these carry echoes of the classical tale of Hades and Persephone, another rather gothic story.

### The Monk

The main narrator in *The Monk* is for once not first person. The two extracts provide different voices, however, and the narrator's own view is hardly objective. The monks' beliefs are called 'Superstition', and the world presented seems to be viewed from a hostile and Protestant perspective. The opening page of the narrative, in fact, argues that Madrid was 'a city where superstition reigns with such despotic sway'. 'Foreign' seems to imply 'corrupt'. The later description of Ambrosio is dominated by negative if rather hyperbolic vocabulary associated with pain and vice: 'selfish', 'crime', 'servile', 'torments', 'damned', etc.

The opening extract delivers an equally extreme view, one that the reader might well suspect will be undermined by events. The emphasis seems to be on sexual virtue, and the descent into sexual corruption does, in fact, come to represent Ambrosio's fall. Interestingly, Ambrosio, like Frankenstein, lacks or loses his parents, and the process of his education is presented as a crucial factor in his eventual destruction. As often, and as in tragedy, fate seems to play a significant part in the lives of these gothic protagonists.

*Summary*

In this chapter you have identified some of the characteristic features of gothic protagonists as revealed in a range of contrasting texts spanning a period of some 200 years. You have learnt that reader response may be influenced by the choice of narrator: either the gothic protagonist her/himself or a passive recorder of events, sharply distinguished in character from the more evil and dangerous protagonist.

# 4 Female characters in gothic texts

*Aims of the chapter:*

- explores the place of women in gothic fiction
- looks at the characteristic features of different female characters
- considers some of the ways in which these characters are presented.

## Two types of female character

Gothic fiction has become a popular area for **feminist** studies. Many commentators, for instance, have noted how females in gothic fiction often fall into one of two categories: the trembling and innocent victim, or the shameless and dangerous **predator**.

### The trembling victim

The trembling victim model is characteristically frail, blonde-haired, a representative of 'respectable' society, largely silent, passive and wide-eyed. Film critics have focused on this example of the female gaze, usually fixed on the monster, as a means of exploring what they see as the gothic-horror's tendency to position the woman as victim.

They have also suggested that the woman's occasional sympathy for the monster may represent the exclusion of both from the power structures of conventional society. In fact this is a question you might ask yourself about any gothic text you read: To what extent are women suppressed or marginalised within the story?

The trembling victim model often appears in the role of the pursued maiden, fleeing a rapacious and predatory male, as we shall see later in this chapter. She may also play the traditional role of the trapped princess, awaiting the saviour prince.

### The predator

The other model of the gothic female is the sharply contrasting figure of the *femme fatale*, memorably parodied by Fenella Fielding in one of the 'Carry On' films, *Carry On Screaming*. This type of female is dark haired, red-lipped, often wears a tight black dress and possesses a startling cleavage. She may be presented more seriously as a dangerous, rapacious creature, offering a very real sexual threat. Such women are often punished within the story for their transgressions. A good example of this occurs in Susan Hill's *The Woman in Black*, where the whole tale revolves around society's punishment of a 'fallen woman'.

### Key terms

**Feminist:** relating to the exploration and interpretation of women's experience within society (or, as here, within a text), and especially a recognition of the historical and cultural subordination of women, and the resolve to do something about it.

**Predator:** something or someone that preys on others.

**Eponymous:** term applied to a central protagonist who gives their name to the title of a text.

### Did you know?

One memorable example of the victim model occurs in the original film version of *King Kong* (1933), where the fragile figure of Fay Wray is famously clasped in the huge fist of the monstrous ape.

## The importance of the female in gothic literature

Mario Pratz, in his introduction to *Three Gothic Novels* (1968), argued that the rise of the Gothic in the 18th century was precisely due to that period's 'feminine character'. There is no doubting the significant role that the female characters play in many gothic texts. It has been argued that the stories play out a battle of the sexes, that they explore the uneasy relationship between pain and love, that the mother figure is a hugely significant presence – or absence. In *Frankenstein* the **eponymous** hero effectively usurps the maternal role of the female in his bringing the creature to life. The women in the novel seem largely helpless creatures, both in terms of the influence they have on others and in their attempts to protect themselves. Significantly, Frankenstein refuses to construct a female partner for his male creation.

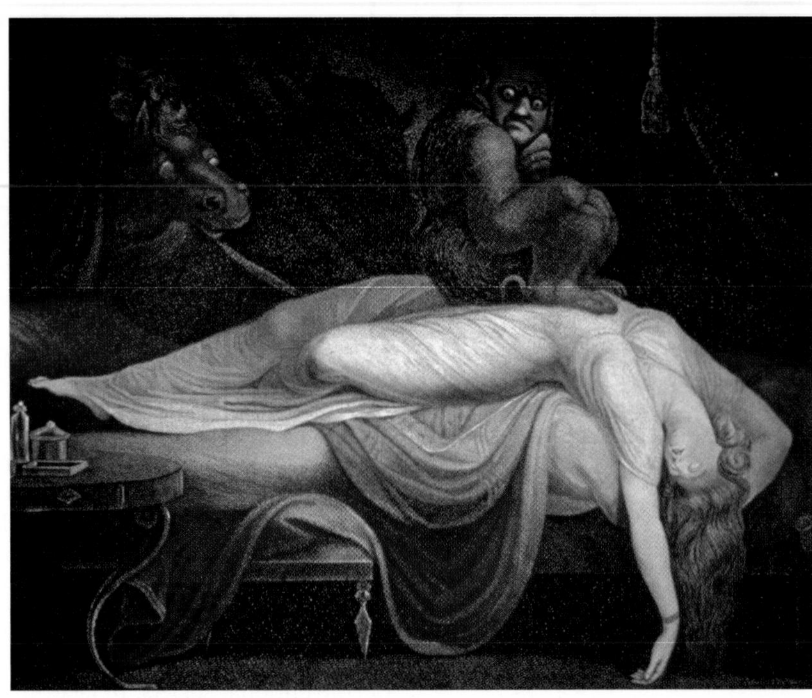

*Henry Fuseli's masterpiece* The Nightmare *has been a famous image of horror ever since it was first exhibited in 1982. Many critics have commented on the ways in which the scene in Fuseli's painting resembles that in Mary Shelley's* Frankenstein *where Frankenstein views the body of his murdered bride.*

### Did you know?

Emily Brontë's novel *Wuthering Heights* had a mixed reception when it was first published in 1847. It certainly achieved far less success than her sister Charlotte's novel *Jane Eyre*. A year later Emily Brontë died of tuberculosis. Since then her novel has become one of the most written-about novels in the English language.

## The expression of feeling

It has frequently been suggested that an important role of the females in gothic texts is to express feeling, often as a means of heightening terror. Consider the following extract from *Wuthering Heights* by Emily Brontë (1847). Catherine Linton, following a confrontation between her husband Edgar and her friend Heathcliff (to whom she has been inseparably attached since childhood), has locked herself in her room. She complains of her husband's cool behaviour to Nelly Dean, the housekeeper. Isabella is Edgar's sister.

> 'If I were only sure it would kill him,' she interrupted, 'I'd kill myself directly! These three awful nights, I've never closed my lids – and oh, I've been tormented! I've been haunted, Nelly! But I begin to fancy you don't like me. How strange! I thought, though everybody hated and despised each other, they could not avoid loving me – and they have all turned to enemies in a few hours. They have, I'm positive; the people here. How dreary to meet death, surrounded by their cold faces! Isabella, terrified and repelled, afraid to enter the room, it would be so dreadful to watch Catherine go. And Edgar standing solemnly by to see it over; then offering prayers of thanks to God for restoring peace to his house and then going back to his books! What in the name of all that feels, has he to do with books, when I am dying?'

***Emily Brontë***, Wuthering Heights, *pp120–1*

### Link

For a commentary on Activity 1, see the end of the chapter.

### Activity 1

In what ways does Catherine express her feelings in the extract? What other gothic elements are present?

### Activity 2

Now carry out a similar analysis of the following passage. Look closely at those words that refer to feeling and consider how the speaker's views and attitudes are presented. In this extract from Mary Shelley's *Frankenstein* the unjustly accused Justine feels her fate is sealed.

There is no commentary on this activity.

> Justine shook her head mournfully. 'I do not fear to die,' she said; 'that pang is past. God raises my weakness and gives me courage to endure the worst. I leave a sad and bitter world; and if you remember me and think of me as one unjustly condemned, I am resigned to the fate awaiting me. Learn from me, dear lady, to submit in patience to the will of heaven!'
>
> ***Mary Shelley***, Frankenstein, *p84*

You may have distinguished the above two passages in terms of the degree of helplessness shown by the female characters.

## Female stereotypes and ambivalence of response

As we noted earlier in this chapter, one of the familiar, stereotypical images of gothic fiction is that of the pursued maiden, fleeing a rapacious and predatory male. However, you may have seen the above passage as being significantly different in this respect from the extract from *Wuthering Heights*. Not all pursuits are performed by men. Certainly, it is hard to view Catherine as a merely passive victim of circumstance. Our response to her predicament is therefore likely to be **ambivalent**.

This ambivalence of response lies at the heart of the experience of reading gothic fiction. The pursued maiden is balanced within gothic narratives by the *femme fatale*. Threatening and dangerous women are a staple part of vampire stories and bring with them unsettling images of sexual aggression and illicit desires. It has often been noted how gothic authors are able to use female characters of this type as a means of exploring material otherwise very much off-limits. It is possible to view the flight of gothic maidens as a fantasy of escape from constraint within a **paternalistic** world. From a similar perspective, the dangerous female characters of gothic texts might represent **emancipated** women, no longer prepared to conform and submit to male control. In John Webster's play *The White Devil* (1612), the female protagonist, Vittoria Corombona, seems to scorn any virtue but courage, and defiantly faces down her male opponents.

At times ambivalence, or uncertainty, can be a very significant part of the threat offered by female gothic characters.

### Key terms

**Ambivalent:** where one person has opposite feelings towards the same object or idea.

**Paternalistic:** like a father; often used to suggest an excessive degree of male power.

**Emancipated:** freed from restraint, usually legal, social or political.

### Activity 3

Read the following passage from Shakespeare's *Macbeth* and consider the significance of the presentation of the female characters. (Here the females are witches whom the soldiers Macbeth and Banquo have met as they return home in triumph after defeating the King's enemies in battle.)

### Link

For a commentary on Activity 3, see the end of the chapter.

### Link

If you can get hold of a copy of *Macbeth*, read a little more of this scene, Act 1 Scene 3 lines 1–88 (the text of *Macbeth* is also available online).

***Macbeth:*** So foul and fair a day I have not seen.
***Banquo:*** How far is't call'd to Forres? – What are these,
So withere'd and so wild in their attire,
That look not like th'inhabitants o'th'earth
And yet are on't. Live you? or are you aught
That man may question? You seem to understand me,
By each at once her choppy finger laying
Upon her skinny lips: you should be women,
And yet your beards forbid me to interpret
That you are so.

Macbeth *1.3 lines 38–47*

*Henry Fuseli's* The Weird Sisters, *1783. What does this interpretation add to your feelings about females in gothic fiction?*

### AQA Examiner's tip

In *Macbeth*, the early appearance of the witches creates an unsettling effect that gradually grows within the play. In your studies always consider the significance of particular sections to the text as a whole.

### Activity 4

1. Read the following description of the vampires from Bram Stoker's novel *Dracula* (1897) and identify what seem to you to be the significant features of their presentation.
2. Look carefully at the nouns that dominate the description.
3. How are feelings and desires carefully balanced here, and what does this tell us about the effect of the vampires on the narrator?

There is no commentary on this activity.

All three had brilliant white teeth, that shone like pearls against the ruby of their voluptuous lips. There was something about them that made me uneasy, some longing and at the same time some deadly fear. I felt in my heart a wicked, burning desire that they would kiss me with those red lips.

***Bram Stoker,*** Dracula, *p53*

## The mother figure

Despite the fact that the dominating father is a key presence in the Gothic, the monstrous mother also plays a prominent part in some gothic narratives. Norman Bates's dead mother in *Psycho* is a notorious cinematic example, but there are many other instances of gothic texts where the mother figure is brought low by one means or another. Frankenstein's usurpation of the role of the mother in Chapter 5 of the novel is an offence against nature, the consequences of which ultimately destroy him and his creation, but other gothic mothers themselves act as destructive characters. They are often presented in such a way as to challenge the stereotypical image of a mother as a comforting, protective figure. In Stephen King's *Carrie* (1974), Carrie's mother's brutal treatment of her daughter proves indirectly responsible for the devastating events that conclude the story.

Angela Carter's 'The Bloody Chamber' provides a rather different perspective on the mother figure. The female narrator's mother is introduced to us early as 'eagle-featured, indomitable' and she reappears at the end of the story in the manner of the knight-errant as the saviour of her daughter.

In *The Monk*, however, the villainous Ambrosio slaughters Antonio's mother as a means of removing possible opposition to his lustful desires. Certainly, one way or another the role and nature of mothers seems to have been a significant feature of gothic writers' treatment of women.

### Extension activities

1. Explore the roles and presentation of women in plays that have gothic qualities. You might consider a range of Shakespearean drama here: *Macbeth*, *Romeo and Juliet* and *Hamlet* are all plays in which women play roles that in some ways match the examples given above.

2. Female characters have occupied a very significant place in gothic films. The following examples offer you some opportunities for comparative study of how women are positioned by the film narrative. (Note that all the films are made by men.)
   - *Frankenstein* (directed by James Whale, 1931): here, and in the numerous sequels, the roles of the women in Frankenstein's life were given added significance.
   - *Dr Jekyll and Mr Hyde* (Robert Mamoulian, 1931): the characters of Champagne Ivy and Muriel provide an interesting contrast in terms of gender roles.
   - *Dracula* (Tod Browning, 1931 and Francis Ford Coppola, 1992): the role played by Winona Ryder in the later version places the female at the heart of the story.
   - *Psycho* (Alfred Hitchcock, 1960): interestingly different forms of sexuality are reflected in the characters of Marion Crane and her sister Lila; there's also, of course, Mother.
   - *Carrie* (Brian de Palma, 1976): there's significant use of the imagery of blood here, menstrual and other.
   - *Alien* (Ridley Scott, 1979) (and the sequels): the film presents a very complex and disturbing view of birth and motherhood.
   - *Interview with the Vampire* (Neil Jordan, 1994): dominated by a rather homoerotic viewpoint, but the portrait of Claudia introduces a different perspective on the gothic female.

## Commentaries

### *Commentary on Activity 1*

- Catherine's speech is studded with questions and exclamations, all contributing to the rather self-consciously theatrical nature of her complaint.
- In a sense, she constructs a little dramatic scene in which all the other characters revolve around her.
- Images of a desired death are set against scornful references to peace and prayer: a use of contrast that characterises much gothic fiction.
- Feelings are extreme: 'tormented', 'hated' and 'despised'.
- The reference to 'haunted' evokes the very gothic sense of a powerful past and also adds to the sense of steadily heightening terror within the chapter.

### *Commentary on Activity 3*

The uncertainty and ambivalence that is so characteristic of the Gothic is revealed here through the way that questions dominate the dialogue. This uncertainty extends to the nature of the witches. What are they? The words that Banquo uses stress the sense of something unnatural: not easily identified in terms of gender, age or even being.

The deep unease that these women engender within a very masculine world emerges through the way they are described: 'choppy finger', 'skinny lips' and 'beards'. The threat they offer to morality is paralleled by the threat that is suggested by a physical appearance that challenges gender conventions. At present they are mysteriously silent, but when they break into speech their menace increases. These seem to be women whose power transcends the physical dominance of the two soldiers.

*Summary*

In this chapter you have explored a number of ways in which female characters operate within a gothic narrative, ranging from the passive, submissive victim to the dangerous predator who offers a sexual threat, and the monstrous mother figure. You have learnt that in gothic literature women often perform the very important role of conveying feelings, and that their physicality is often stressed, whether for positive or negative effect.

# 5 Gothic drama

*Aims of the chapter:*

- looks at the dramatic qualities of gothic texts
- explores some gothic aspects of Shakespeare's plays
- considers gothic elements in other Elizabethan and Jacobean plays.

The popular use of the term 'dramatic', tends to refer to something excessive, unexpected, or even shocking. The word 'drama' comes from the Greek verb 'to do', *dran*; thus the idea of action is made central to drama. This sense of something action-packed, arresting and extreme is central to the elements of the Gothic you have explored so far. It is not surprising, therefore, to find that the cinema and the theatre are places where the Gothic has had an enduring appeal. The intensity of the gothic experience might also seem to create a natural alliance with a medium where concentration is a necessity because of the limitations in time and space of a dramatic performance.

Drama involves illusion, an audience's conscious acceptance of artifice. Acting involves someone pretending to be what they are not, adopting a role, playing a part. These factors suggest that drama naturally lends itself to the exploration of gothic tales in which characters constantly dissemble, deceive and disguise themselves.

Melodrama, with its tendency to deal in extremes of action, conflict and character, might also seem well suited to the telling of gothic tales. Certainly popular melodramas of the late 19th century such as *Maria Marten, or The Murder in the Red Barn* and *Sweeney Todd, the Demon Barber of Fleet Street* have many of the macabre characteristics of the Gothic.

### Activity 1

**The main elements of drama might be described as: time, place, character, action and audience. Bearing this in mind, take any gothic tale that you know well and plan a dramatic adaptation, including scripting one important scene. Make a note of the material you choose to keep from the original text, and the nature of the changes or emphases you make in order to create an effective piece of gothic drama.**

The popularity of gothic drama is demonstrated both by the number of adaptations of gothic novels in the late 18th and early 19th centuries and also by the original pieces of gothic theatre that were created at that time. Walpole's *The Castle of Otranto* was dramatised under a different title in 1781, and Lewis's *The Monk* likewise in 1798. Richard Brinsley Peake was one of the first in a long line of writers to adapt Mary Shelley's *Frankenstein* for the stage. His play *Presumption; or The Fate of Frankenstein* was performed in London in 1823. For some time gothic drama dominated the popular English stage: contemporary records suggest that an average of four new gothic plays were produced each year during the last decade of the 18th century.

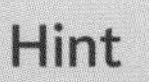

### Hint

It should be remembered that in a sense the term 'gothic' has to be applied retrospectively to Shakespearean drama and other 16th- and 17th-century plays, in that the generic term was not widely used until some time later.

## Shakespeare and the Gothic

The importance of Shakespeare to the gothic genre can be illustrated by noting the number of direct or indirect references to Shakespearean plays within gothic texts. During the 18th century Shakespeare also came to increasingly represent or symbolise something essentially English, representing a combination of the best from the native tradition (often

## Remember

The **Renaissance** is the period of European history from approximately 1550 to 1660.

## Key terms

**Reformation:** religious movement of 16th-century Europe to reform the Roman Catholic Church. It resulted in the establishment of the Reformed and Protestant Churches.

## Did you know?

David Garrick (1717–79) dominated the theatre of his day as actor, dramatist and theatre manager. One of his significant innovations was to ban a practice that had continued since Elizabethan times, of allowing spectators on the stage itself.

## Link

For a commentary on Activity 2, see the end of the chapter.

linked to the medieval Gothic) and the new independence of thought and belief that accompanied the English Renaissance and **Reformation** in the 16th century. The fame of the actor David Garrick was due in no small degree to his nerve-tingling performances in scenes of supernatural terror from plays such as *Macbeth* and *Richard III*.

## Activity 2

Read the following short extracts from *Richard III*, *Hamlet* and *Macbeth*. What do gothic features contribute to the dramatic effect of the scenes? Note that all three extracts involve a confrontation between the central protagonist and the supernatural.

### *Richard III*

A series of ghosts have appeared to Richard on the night before the Battle of Bosworth, bidding him 'despair and die'. The King wakes in sudden fear.

#### From Act 5 Scene 3

***Richard:*** Give me another horse! Bind up my wounds!
Have mercy, Jesu! – Soft! I did but dream.
O coward conscience, how dost thou afflict me!
The lights burn blue. It is now dead midnight.
Cold fearful drops stand on my trembling flesh.
What do I fear? Myself? There's none else by.
Richard loves Richard: that is, I am I.
Is there a murderer here? No. Yes, I am.
Then fly. What, from myself? Great reason why –
Lest I revenge. Myself upon myself?
Alack, I love myself. Wherefore? For any good
That I myself have done unto myself?
O no! Alas, I rather hate myself
For hateful deeds committed by myself.

Richard III *5.3, lines 178–91*

### *Hamlet*

Hamlet meets the ghost of his dead father on the castle battlements.

#### From Act 1 Scene 4

***Hamlet:*** Angels and ministers of grace defend us!
Be thou a spirit of health or goblin damned,
Bring with thee airs from heaven or blasts from hell,
Be thy intents wicked or charitable
Thou comest in such a questionable shape
That I will speak to thee. I'll call thee Hamlet,
King, Father, Royal Dane. O, answer me!
Let me not burst in ignorance; but tell
Why thy canonized bones, hears'd in death,
Have burst their cerements; why the sepulchre
Wherein we saw thee quietly inurned
Hath oped his ponderous and marble jaws
To cast thee up again!

Hamlet *1.4, lines 39–51*

## *Macbeth*

The ghost of Banquo appears to Macbeth at a banquet.

### From Act 3 Scene 4

***Macbeth:*** Which of you have done this?<br>
**Lords:** What, my good Lord?<br>
***Macbeth:*** Thou canst not say, I did it: never shake<br>
Thy gory locks at me.<br>
***Ross:*** Gentlemen, rise; his Highness is not well.<br>
***Lady Macbeth:*** Sit, worthy friends. My Lord is often thus,<br>
And hath been from his youth: pray you, keep seat;<br>
The fit is momentary; upon a thought<br>
He will again be well. If much you note him,<br>
You shall offend him, and extend his passion;<br>
Feed and regard him not. – Are you a man?<br>
***Macbeth:*** Ay, and a bold one, that dare look on that<br>
Which might appal the Devil.<br>
***Lady Macbeth:*** O proper stuff!<br>
This is the very painting of your fear:<br>
This is the air-drawn dagger, which, you said,<br>
Led you to Duncan. O! these flaws and starts<br>
(Imposters to true fear), would well become<br>
A woman's story at a winter's fire,<br>
Authoriz'd by her grandma. Shame itself!<br>
Why do you make such faces? When all's done,<br>
You look but on a stool.<br>
***Macbeth:*** Pr'ythee, see there!<br>
Behold! Look! Lo! How say you?<br>
Why, what care I? If thou canst nod, speak too –<br>
If charnel-houses and our graves must send<br>
Those that we bury, back, our monuments<br>
Shall be the maws of kites.

*Macbeth* *3.4, lines 47–72*

### Extension activity

Do some further reading of one of these three plays to gain more detailed understanding of the central protagonist. 'Hot-seat' the chosen main character as a means of exploring their motivations and mixed senses of guilt and defiance.

## Elizabethan and Jacobean drama

English drama in the late Elizabethan and **Jacobean** periods had many of the qualities that characterise the Gothic. Many plays were preoccupied with mortality and the constant presence of death. There was a strong sense of the darkness within the human soul and the presence of evil in the world. Dramatists took as their themes family discord, power struggles, sin and damnation. Many, including Shakespeare, combined tragic and comic effects within their plays. This broke with the rules of classical drama, but enabled writers to explore extremes of feeling and strongly contrasting effects.

### AQA Examiner's tip

Drama, itself a genre, has its own methods and conventions. When exploring drama texts make sure that you treat the texts as drama, plays written for performance, and not as though they were novels or biographies.

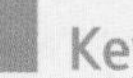

### Key terms

**Jacobean:** the period of the reign of King James I, 1603–25.

### Link

For a commentary on Activity 3, see opposite.

### Activity 3

Read the following two soliloquies. The first is taken from the end of Christopher Marlowe's *Dr Faustus* (1604), where Faustus awaits his terrible fate. Faustus has bargained away his soul in exchange for twenty-four years of luxurious living and the constant service of the devil Mephistopheles. The time has come, and Mephistopheles is about to arrive and carry him off to Hell. The second soliloquy comes from *The Revenger's Tragedy*, probably by Thomas Middleton (1607). Vindice, the revenger of the title, addresses the skull of his murdered mistress. In what ways do the two passages deal with the idea of death?

**Faustus** The stars move still, time runs, the clock will strike,
The devil will come, and Faustus must be damned.
O, I'll leap up to my God! Who pulls me down?
See, see where Christ's blood streams in the firmament!
One drop would save my soul, half a drop. Ah, my Christ!–
Rend not my heart for naming of my Christ;
Yet will I call on him. O spare me, Lucifer! –

Dr Faustus *5.2, lines 143–9*

**Vindice** And now methinks I could e'en chide myself
For doting on her beauty, though her death
Shall be revenged after no common action.
Does the silkworm expend her yellow labours
For thee? For thee does she undo herself?
Are lordships sold to maintain ladyships
For the poor benefit of a bewitching minute? ...

Surely we're all mad people and they,
Whom we think are, are not: we mistake those.
'Tis we are mad in sense, they but in clothes.

The Revenger's Tragedy *3.5, lines 68–74, 79–81*

### Extension activity

Read the Jacobean play *The White Devil* by John Webster. Consider the dramatic methods through which the play deals with power, sin, and the constant presence of death within a corrupt and self-seeking society.

The Garden of Earthly Delights *by Hieronymus Bosch*

## Commentaries

### *Commentary on Activity 2*

One distinction that you might have made is regarding the degree of guilt shown by the characters in connection with the appearance of the ghost. A guilty response to such visitations is standard fare in many early gothic novels. Macbeth and Richard are forced to endure the appearance of spirits of those they have slain, showing a mixture of guilty confession and bold defiance. In fact, you might find an interesting progression here in Shakespeare's presentation of Richard, an earlier creation, to the more complex figure of Macbeth. Hamlet, in contrast, sees in the ghost possible answers to the uncertainties that have been torturing him.

Both Hamlet and Macbeth see something unnatural in the appearance of a body from beyond the grave, but this in itself signifies the importance of the appearance of the ghost both to the speaker and to the audience. The 'charnel-house', 'grave' and 'sepulchre' are all familiar elements of the gothic scene.

A significant difference between the three extracts is that the last involves dramatic dialogue, whereas the first and second are **soliloquies**. You might consider to what extent the soliloquy is naturally suited to the gothic genre, in the opportunities it provides for a character's extended soul-searching. The style of the two soliloquies is markedly different. Hamlet's speech is more ordered in its **rhetorical** patterns and **syntax**, despite the exclamatory nature of much of his language. The contrasting imagery of Heaven and Hell is typical of gothic balancing of opposites, as is the use of **personification** in reference to the buildings associated with death.

Richard's speech is far more broken and disjointed; the patterns of what is a sort of internal dialogue are cruder and more abrupt, reflecting his anguished state of mind. The vocabulary of fear, dream, conscience and murder is very gothic, however, as is Richard's obsessive self-reference. It is characteristic of the gothic villain to engage in tortured self-examination as the day of their doom draws near.

The extract from *Macbeth* reveals another characteristic of the Gothic: its fondness for **metafiction** and **intertextuality**. Lady Macbeth describes her husband's behaviour as worthy of 'a woman's story at a winter's fire', thus drawing attention to the fictional nature of the play itself. Interestingly, she associates Macbeth's terror with female behaviour, here and in her question 'Are you a man?' You may wish to consider whether this view is characteristic of the female perspective within the Gothic, explored in Chapter 4 of this unit.

### Key terms

**Soliloquy:** a speech given by a character alone on the stage, in which they tell or confess their thoughts to the audience.

**Personification:** where human qualities are attributed to non-human things.

**Metafiction:** fiction that is about fiction; stories that draw attention to their own fictional status.

**Intertextuality:** the ways in which texts refer to other texts.

## *Commentary on Activity 3*

In the first passage Faustus struggles in vain against oncoming death, the punishment he has brought upon himself. Earlier in the play his pride and overreaching lust for knowledge and power have been vividly displayed. Now he is doomed because of the terrible bargain he has made with Lucifer, to whom at intervals he directly speaks. (It is easy to see Mary Shelley's debt to Marlowe in her portrait of Frankenstein.) The stress on time emphasises the inevitable outcome. Death will bring eternal damnation, not the hope of paradise. Images of blood here represent the possible salvation Faustus has scorned.

The tone of the second passage is more ironic, however bitter. A physical symbol of death, the skull, is addressed in knowing and disillusioned terms. The bare, uncompromising skull reveals in itself the shallowness and brevity of earthly desires. (It will also shortly be directly used, in a very gothic manner, as a means of poisoning one of Vindice's enemies.) Further contemplation suggests to Vindice that society confuses the sane and insane: it is a sign of madness to believe in nothing but earthly power and pleasure. (Look at the character of Renfield in Stoker's *Dracula* as a further example of how gothic writers are able to use the idea of madness in their stories.)

*Summary*

In this chapter you have seen that the gothic genre has many features that suit dramatic presentation, and that melodrama has many gothic characteristics. You have learnt that many Shakespeare plays contain material that we associate with the Gothic, in terms of character, action and setting; and that Elizabethan and Jacobean drama as a whole is often gothic in character. You have studied these gothic elements in extracts from a number of plays.

# 6 Different ways of looking at gothic texts

*Aims of the chapter:*

- considers some critical perspectives on gothic texts
- looks at some aspects of narrative structures
- debates whether or not the Gothic can be seen as a serious literary genre.

## Key terms

**Subverted:** undermined by a particular perception or reality.

**Marginal:** on the margins, not central.

## Critical perspectives

You should by now have realised that any definition of a genre cannot be absolutely precise or final. Like other genres, the Gothic operates through a series of familiar elements. These elements may vary from text to text, but a sufficient number will be constant enough to permit a form of loose classification. Once a genre becomes established it is likely to be constantly revised, **subverted** or even parodied. Also, like any literary form, gothic fiction resists any one reading. Different critical approaches can allow you to explore new interpretations of familiar texts.

### Feminist readings

Chapter 4, on women in gothic fiction, indicated some ways in which gender issues within the texts might be explored. Some feminist critics have suggested that gothic texts frequently explore the conflict between the sexes, either directly or through more complex, symbolic means. The gothic castle, for instance, through which the pursued female victim desperately flees, has been seen as representing the limited domestic world in which 18th- and 19th-century women were trapped.

The general absence or marginalisation of women in texts such as Stevenson's *Dr Jekyll and Mr Hyde* has often been noted, and has led some critics to argue that the associations between the men themselves shadow male–female relationships. Elaine Showalter, in *Sexual Anarchy: Gender and Culture at the Fin de Siècle* (1990), has seen Hyde as the embodiment of society's fears of what was then illegal homosexuality. Hyde flaunts his debaucheries in a world where the other characters either practise rigorous self-denial or seek their pleasures in secret.

Angela Carter famously claimed 'We live in Gothic times', thus indicating how once **marginal** genres can come to establish themselves in the mainstream culture. In her story 'The Bloody Chamber', she offers the reader the familiar gothic trappings of a fearful bride at the mercy of a vampiric husband within a dark castle. The 17-year-old girl disobeys her absent husband, 'like Eve', we are told, when she opens the door to a forbidden room, hoping to 'find a little of his soul'. What she finds is a horrific torture chamber where the bodies of her husband's previous wives lie. Here, as elsewhere in the story, women's sexual relations with men are associated with images of suffering and pain.

> 'There is a striking resemblance between the act of love and the ministrations of a torturer,' opined my husband's favourite poet; I had learned something of the nature of that similarity on my marriage bed. And now my taper showed me the outlines of a rack. There was also a great wheel, like the ones I had seen in woodcuts of the martyrdom of the saints, in my old nurse's little store of holy books. And – just one glimpse of it before my little flame caved in and I was left in absolute darkness – a metal figure, hinged at the side, which I knew to be spiked on the inside and to have the name: the Iron Maiden.

***Angela Carter**, 'The Bloody Chamber', p27*

You may feel that much of the language of this extract portrays women in the traditional gothic position of submission and vulnerability, but note how in the climax of the tale Carter dramatically subverts the convention with the triumphant re-entrance into the story of the bride's mother.

> You never saw such a wild thing as my mother, her hat seized by the winds and blown out to sea so that her hair was her white mane, her black lisle legs exposed to the thigh, her skirts tucked round her waist, one hand on the reins of the rearing horse while the other clasped my father's service revolver and, behind her, the breakers of the savage, indifferent sea, like the witnesses of a furious justice.
>
> *'The Bloody Chamber', p39*

### Activity 1

**In what ways does the language of this second extract challenge the traditional expectations of female behaviour?**

### Link

For a commentary on Activity 1, see the end of the chapter.

Sandra Gilbert and Susan Gubar, in their essay 'Mary Shelley's Monstrous Eve' from *The Madwoman in the Attic* (1979), have argued a reading of *Frankenstein* that sees the novel as a parody of *Paradise Lost*, but one in which both the Monster and Frankenstein in different ways represent the character of Eve. Thus, instead of seeing the female characters as passive, largely helpless figures within the novel, we are given a reading that repositions women's experience at the heart of the narrative. Frankenstein, from this perspective, gives birth to the monster; his anguished drudgery in his workshop represents labour pains, and his lust for forbidden knowledge parallels Eve's fatal bite of the apple.

## Marxist readings

A **Marxist** interpretation of a text is driven by the idea that the text is significantly tied to its social and political contexts. In the late 18th century the Marquis de Sade famously argued that the Gothic 'was the inevitable product of the revolutionary shocks which afflicted the whole of Europe'. De Sade's suggestion was that the horrific conditions of the time were such that literature was itself driven to extremes in order to make an impact. You may have noted also how many of the villains of the early gothic novels are from aristocratic backgrounds. At a time of the growth of the shift towards a more commercially driven, bourgeois society, the aristocracy was often viewed as corrupt, parasitic and given to a life of self-indulgence.

But the gothic world can also be used to highlight the faults of the post-feudal, industrial society. The figure of the vampire may be taken, through a Marxist reading, to represent the insatiable greed of capitalism, feeding off the bodies of its workers. The nightmare world of Mervyn Peake's *Gormenghast* trilogy is often thought to be a response to the later horrors of the mid-20th century.

Mary Shelley's *Frankenstein* serves as an example of how you may interpret a text through a Marxist reading. If, for instance, the Monster is taken to represent the increasingly politically conscious working classes, then is the portrait sympathetic, as Mary Shelley's radical background might lead us to expect, or hostile and fearful of the powers of the mob? A similar ambivalence of response may be found in Frankenstein's own wavering feelings when his creation begs him to 'create a female for me'.

### Key terms

**Marxist:** there are many aspects to Marxism, but essentially it describes social change in terms of economic factors. It is especially interested, therefore, in aspects of power.

### Did you know?

The name of the Marquis De Sade (1740–1814) is notoriously associated with cruel and unnatural sexual practices, giving rise to the word 'sadism'. He was for a time an army officer and was imprisoned in the Bastille, where he wrote many books, some reflecting the political and philosophical controversies of the day.

### Remember

**Ambivalence of response** was discussed in Chapter 4.

### Did you know?

The German political and economic theorist Karl Marx (1818–83) was the intellectual force behind modern communism. He spent much of his later life in exile in London, where he is buried, in Highgate Cemetery.

### Key terms

**Alienated:** made to feel distanced, isolated, even hostile.

> His words had a strange effect on me. I compassionated him and sometimes felt a wish to console him; but when I looked upon him, when I saw the filthy mass that moved and talked, my heart sickened and my feelings were altered to those of horror and hatred.
>
> ***Mary Shelley***, Frankenstein, *p.142*

### Activity 2

In *Frankenstein*, or in any other gothic text with which you are familiar, what evidence can you find for seeing the 'monster' as a representative of an **alienated**, subordinated figure in a world dominated by rigid class divisions?

Another significant social and economic context at the time of Mary Shelley's novel was the growth in scientific knowledge and discovery. The potential power thus made available was a cause of much excitement, but also much unease. Here is Frankenstein, close to the completion of his second creation, but racked with doubts as to whether his scientific enquiries will ultimately have horrendous consequences.

> In the mean time I worked on, and my labour was already considerably advanced. I looked towards its completion with a tremulous and eager hope, which I dared not trust myself to question, but which was intermixed with obscure forebodings of evil, that made my heart sicken in my bosom.
>
> ***Mary Shelley***, Frankenstein, *p.159*

### Activity 3

Discuss whether you feel that in the 21st century we are more or less likely to fear the consequences of scientific research. Does this affect our readings of such novels as *Frankenstein*?

## Religious readings

### Did you know?

Charles Darwin (1809–82) is best known for his development of the theory of evolution by natural selection. His great work *The Origin of Species* argued the case that humans were developed from earlier anthropoid groups.

By the time of Stevenson's *Dr Jekyll and Mr Hyde*, another significant scientific development, Darwinism, had posed a challenge to conventional religious thought. Darwin's theories had dealt a blow to the complacent view of a humankind made in the image of God, and established a disturbing link between humanity and the beast that lay behind them within.

Gothic literature had always operated in a religious context. The fondness for the exploration of the supernatural could be regarded as a quest for a form of religious experience in an increasingly secular age. The worlds of *The Castle of Otranto* and *The Monk* are deliberately placed in the Catholic societies of southern Europe, and tone is often unambiguously anti-Catholic, presenting the rituals of the Church as corrupt and superstitious. There is also, however, a barely concealed fascination with the formality and rituals associated with the Church, which add a sense of grandeur and power to the tales themselves.

In *Frankenstein* the whole novel turns on the mysteries of creation, and Frankenstein's arrogant design to usurp that god-like power. From this come the many parallels with Milton's *Paradise Lost* and the novel's agonised epigraph:

Did I request thee, maker, from my clay
To mould me man? Did I solicit thee
From darkness to promote me?

## Psychological readings

Just as the work of Darwin transformed late 19th-century scientific thinking, so that of Sigmund Freud changed for ever the world of psychology and psychoanalysis. Many of the central components of Freud's theories are also familiar features of gothic tales.

### Did you know?

Sigmund Freud (1856–1939) was one of the founders of modern psychoanalysis. His famous work *The Interpretation of Dreams* argues that in our dreams repressed sexual desires emerge.

### Activity 4

**Consider two or more of the elements of psychological study set out below and apply them to *Frankenstein*, earlier extracts from this chapter, or any other gothic text with which you are familiar.**

### *Elements of psychological study*

1. **The power and appeal of the irrational:** Look at the *Macbeth* extract (the appearance of the witches in Act 1 Scene 3) on p22.
2. **Dreams**, especially those in which subconscious desires swim to the surface: For instance, the extract from *Wuthering Heights* in Chapter 4 is taken from a part of the story where Catherine drifts in a sort of trance between states of consciousness and unconsciousness. Frankenstein falls into a feverish dream at the conclusion of his labours to create the Monster (Volume 1, Chapter 5). Harker experiences an unsettling dream of the vampires in the extract from *Dracula* on p22.
3. **The ways in which illicit desires are controlled and suppressed:** In gothic texts such desires may be satisfied vicariously through the actions of 'monsters' who are then destroyed and thus safely dealt with. From another perspective, this function of the monster may explain the degree to which you may find yourself sympathising with the monster figure.
4. **The mixed response to sexual activity:** Ambrosio, in *The Monk*, is an excellent example of this alternation of attraction and repulsion.
5. **The feeling of guilt:** Which gothic characters seem to you to be particularly affected by this emotion? What causes the guilt?
6. **The complex relationship between parents and children:** You may feel the **Oedipus complex** is a significant force here. Look also at the number of authoritative father figures in gothic texts. How many need to be overthrown? In some cases what is significant is the absence of a stable family environment. Ghostly **revenants** may take their place. Other characters may assume a position of authority in the place of the absent father. You might feel that Frankenstein himself assumes the paternal role, with disastrous results.
7. **The double:** Gothic fiction is dominated by a sense of opposites. Thus characters like Jekyll and Hyde, Frankenstein and the Monster, Dracula and Van Helsing, can be regarded as examples of the divided self, two beings who only exist in terms of the other. You may see some characters, like Faustus, as carrying this division within themselves. You may also wish to consider the relevance of such Freudian concepts as the 'id', the unconscious emotions and desires; the 'ego', the conscious will; and the 'super-ego', the controlling moral force. It is the clash between these functions of the mind that produces much activity within the gothic world.

### Key terms

**Oedipus complex:** a term from psychoanalysis referring to the suppressed desire of a son for his mother or a daughter for her father, considered by Freud to be a normal part of child development. Jealousy of the other parent figure derives from these desires.

**Revenant:** someone who returns (from the dead).

## Looking at narrative structures

The concept of 'the double' also points to characteristic structural patterns within gothic fiction. The Gothic has at times been criticised for what was seen as its incident-driven, sensational plots, especially when contrasted with the forms of **classical** narrative. However, you have seen above the way that gothic fiction uses the idea of opposites, balanced concepts that define each other.

### Key terms

**Classical:** here meaning traditional, based on conventional forms and a sense of order, harmony and proportion.

**Duplicity:** of a deceptive nature, capable of double, or multiple, meanings.

**Trauma:** state of shock.

**Chronologically:** in a time sequence following the order in which events occurred.

### Activity 5

Look at the following patterns and consider their relevance to any gothic text you know well.

- Life and death
- Civilisation and barbarism
- The domestic and the wild
- The natural and the supernatural
- The real and the imaginary
- Reason and passion

This interest in the double may explain the fondness of gothic fiction for the double (or multiple) narrative. There are (at least) three narrators in *Frankenstein*. There are several narrative voices in Chaucer's *The Pardoner's Tale*. What do you feel is the impact of this narrative device on your reading of these stories or any other multiple-narrative gothic tale? It has been argued that the use of double voices helps to add to the sense of ambiguity and confusion that characterises the genre.

Consider also the following features of gothic narratives.

### *The sense of the problematic nature of narrative itself*

Many narrators are self-conscious, aware of the **duplicity** of narrative, at pains to justify their story. Look at the similarities between these two extracts from Anne Rice's *Interview with the Vampire* (1976) and Coleridge's *The Rime of the Ancient Mariner*.

> The vampire clamped a hand on the boy's shoulder and said, 'believe me, I won't hurt you. I want this opportunity. It's more important to me than you can realise now. I want you to begin.' And he withdrew his hand and sat collected, waiting.

***Anne Rice**, Interview with the Vampire, p6*

> Since then, at an uncertain hour,
> That agony returns:
> And till my ghastly tale is told
> This heart within me burns.

***Samuel Taylor Coleridge**, The Rime of the Ancient Mariner, Part 7*

### *The question of time within the narrative*

The Gothic places a great deal of emphasis on the question of time within the narrative. Consider whether the plots of the texts you know are driven by past **trauma** and a response to a significant past event.

### *Change and transformation*

Gothic fiction is characterised by sudden changes and transformations. There may be regular breaks in the narrative and events may not unfold **chronologically**.

### *Beginnings and endings*

Significant use may be made of the beginning and the end of the narrative. The tale may achieve 'closure' through the defeat of evil. More modern gothic tales often resist such comforting conclusions. The gothic protagonists may not be so easily categorised as objects of fear and loathing; society may not be returned to its former stability.

### Activity 6

Consider the above narrative elements in relation to any gothic text that you have read.

**AQA Examiner's tip**

When exploring a writer's method, don't become over-concerned with minor details of language. Always also look at the larger narrative structures within the text.

## Is the Gothic a serious genre?

### No?

Much early comment on the gothic genre represented it as mere self-indulgence and excess. Formless and vulgar by the standards of 18th-century neo-classical taste, its plots were considered absurd and its moral view suspect. Henry Tilney's retort to Catherine Morland in *Northanger Abbey* may be taken as an example of the suspicion that was felt towards the feelings engendered by gothic fiction.

**Remember**

**Neo-classicism** was defined in Chapter 2.

> 'Dear Miss Morland, consider the dreadful nature of the suspicions you have entertained. What have you been judging from? Remember the country and the age in which we live. Remember that we are English, that we are Christians. Consult your own understanding, your own sense of the probable, your own observation of what is passing around you –'
>
> ***Jane Austen***, Northanger Abbey, *p186*

Even in modern times critics have given the genre no more than faint praise:

> Although the literary quality of the tales of terror is not very high, we must agree with Dr Lundblad that the Gothic romance grew into one of the most powerful currents in the general literature of the nineteenth century.
>
> ***Mario Praz***, Introduction to Three Gothic Novels *(1968), p34*

### Yes?

More recently there have been more positive assessments. Fred Botting has argued for the enduring relevance of the Gothic in contemporary culture:

> Gothic representations are a product of cultural anxieties about the nature of human identity, the stability of cultural formations, and processes of change … They retain a double function in simultaneously assuaging and intensifying the anxieties with which they engage. Hence the persistence of Gothic throughout the 200-year period associated with modernity.
>
> *From* The Cambridge Companion to Gothic Fiction *(2002), p280*

In changing times, a narrative form that confronts the consequences of loss of faith, and questions the established notions of social order and justice, can always lay claim to continued relevance. In traumatic periods of history, traumatised heroes may represent contemporary uncertainties and insecurities. Again in changing times, a genre that deals so frequently with **metamorphosis** is likely to prove attractive.

### Key terms

**Metamorphosis:** a transformation; something or someone undergoes a change in form or appearance.

## Key points to remember

- The Gothic is a hybrid form. It draws ideas and inspiration from Shakespeare and medieval ballads, from folklore and scientific speculation. In this lies its further strength. Modern forms of the Gothic include cartoons and comic television parodies, a profusion of graphic novels and an apparently endless desire to reinterpret the tales of Dracula and Frankenstein through film.
- The Gothic explores the nature of narrative itself, creating and exploring its own distinctive features of fear and alienation. Readers and audiences of the Gothic find themselves safely positioned spectators, observing representations of terror where the victim is someone else, but constantly invited to identify with the central protagonists and question their own morality.
- The Gothic seems embedded in our culture. A glance down the columns of television programme schedules for any week in the year will testify to its enduring popularity, as will the town of Whitby, whose twice-yearly gothic festivals have helped propel it into the top handful of tourist attractions in Britain.

### AQA Examiner's tip

Your own response to a text is important. Your exploration of other readers' views and your consideration of their strengths and weaknesses should lead you to your own independent interpretation of the text.

### Extension activity

1. With close reference to any gothic text of your choice, argue the case that the Gothic is more than a light-hearted literary form.
2. Create an itinerary for a literary 'gothic' tour of Britain and Ireland. Choose a range of authors and identify their place in the gothic tradition.

## Commentaries

### *Commentary on Activity 1*

The mother is associated with the power of the elements, especially the sea and the wind. Her actions represent a freedom from convention – 'skirts tucked round her waist' – and she exercises a physical control more usually associated with masculine figures: 'one hand on the reins of the rearing horse'.

*Summary*

In this chapter you have considered a range of critical perspectives on gothic texts, including feminist, Marxist, religious and psychological readings, and have looked at some features of gothic narrative structure. In considering whether the Gothic can be seen as a serious literary genre you have learnt that it has often been viewed as a minor literary form, characterised by excess and lack of control, but that more recent readings have stressed its relevance to modern times and praised its diversity and flexibility.

# 7 The pastoral genre

*Aims of the chapter:*

- introduces aspects of the Pastoral
- explores some different pastoral texts
- identifies some characteristic features of the pastoral genre.

## Activity 1

Find a newspaper or magazine that provides television schedules for the week. List all the programmes for two or three days that seem to have a clear connection with the British countryside, and thus might be considered to be 'pastoral'. Accepting that some programmes may be less familiar to you, try to decide what use they make of their pastoral connections.

- Are there common features?
- Do the programmes cross television genre boundaries?
- How do they seem to *use* their pastoral settings?

When you have completed the task, read the commentary below to see what another group of students discovered.

### *Commentary on Activity 1*

In response to this task, one group of students selected the following list of programmes from a three-day period: *Midsomer Murders*, *Heartbeat*, *Lewis* (a follow-up to *Inspector Morse*), *The Good Life*, *The Vicar of Dibley*, *Countryfile*, *Natural World*, *Escape to the Country*, *Emmerdale*, *Shaun the Sheep*, and *The Trees That Made Britain.*

Your list may well be more comprehensive, but the above selection seems fairly representative of the range of programme types that benefit from a pastoral setting: crime dramas, soaps, sitcoms, children's programmes, and obviously those directly concerned with wildlife.

The students went on to consider what these settings brought to the programmes. One thing they noticed was the number of crime and detection dramas that were set in the country. The group felt that the largely peaceful rural setting acted as a counterpoint, a balance to the violent incidents that disrupted that peace. In general, also, the setting provided a sense of security and continuity to which the characters could retreat after the temporary breach caused by a criminal act.

Different types of programme, of course, have different needs, and you may have discovered very different patterns. Certainly, however, the appeal of the Pastoral within our culture is not restricted to television. The success of the long-running (since 1950!) radio series *The Archers* can in part be attributed to the appeal of its country setting, even (or especially?) to a predominantly urban listenership. The American film *Brokeback Mountain* presented the slow growth of a sexual relationship between two modern-day cowboys, in which the wilderness of their working world provided a liberating contrast to the drab and sterile urban life they had left behind, and offered a largely protective, isolated environment in which their love could flourish.

So there is plenty of evidence that the pastoral ideal has a continued relevance within our modern culture. It is worth, at this point, looking at the various ways in which the term has been defined, and some key terms associated with the Pastoral.

## The meaning of 'pastoral'

A crucially important aspect of the word's meaning is 'pertaining to shepherds'. This can be understood in two importantly distinctive ways.

The *Oxford English Dictionary* gives the following definitions:

1 Of or pertaining to shepherds or their occupation
2 Of land or country: used for pasture
3 Having the simplicity or natural charm associated with such country.

The third definition in particular may be one that you recognised or adopted in completing the task above. The *OED*, however, also offers another definition:

4 Of or pertaining to a pastor or shepherd of souls.

Here the term operates within another, very significant, frame of reference, that of religion. Later you will explore how the pastoral genre includes a religious element, in particular the idea of the Garden of Eden.

The pastoral vision celebrates the virtues of a simple, even unsophisticated, life far away from the city or court. Nostalgia for the past is a dominant idea and this, when linked to the religious perspective indicated above, leads to a longing for a rural paradise representing the Garden of Eden before the fall. Thus the Pastoral may be involved in a search for a lost innocence, perhaps a time when men and women lived in harmony with nature. You will look in more detail at this aspect of the Pastoral later in this unit.

### AQA Examiner's tip

Remember that a literary term may have more than one definition. Always be alert to the possibility of different interpretations of a word.

### Did you know?

One of the earliest and most famous pastoral writers was the Roman poet Virgil (70–19 BC). He is most famous for his epic poem the *Aeneid*, but early works such as the *Eclogues* and the *Georgics* explored different aspects of Italian country life.

### Activity 2

'Nature' is itself a word with many associations and meanings. Make a list of phrases including the word 'nature', and consider the various different ways in which the word is used.

### Link

For a commentary on Activity 2, see the end of the chapter.

**The vocabulary of the Pastoral**

Here are some other terms that you may find useful in your study of the pastoral genre. You will encounter some of these later in this unit.

|  |  |
|---|---|
| **Arcadia** | From the name of a mountainous region in the Peloponnese, Greece. In classical literature it stood for an ideal world of rural tranquillity, where shepherds and shepherdesses minded their flocks far away from the pressures of 'real life'. |
| **Bucolic** | Another term for pastoral, from the Greek word for a herdsman. |
| **Doric** | Rustic. Often used in reference to rough rural manners or dialect as opposed to the sophisticated and urbane. The word comes from 'Doris', a region of Greece south of Thessaly. |
| **Eclogue** | A short poem, often in the form of a pastoral dialogue or part of a longer poem. |
| **Elegy** | Usually a poem of mourning for an individual or tragic event. Pastoral elegies lament the death of a shepherd (or someone represented by the figure of a shepherd), and often follow a series of poetic conventions, one of which is the sense of renewal and hope at the end of the poem. Later versions tended to stress that the pastoral idyll evoked could not be recovered. |
| **Georgic** | A poem about rural life, the main purpose of which is to give practical advice about agricultural matters. |
| **Idyll** | Commonly used to describe a state or scene of tranquil happiness. It can be a poem, a part of a poem or a description of a particular scene. In contrast to the elegy, an idyll presents a positive vision, and one that is attainable. |

### Hint

These definitions suggest that the Pastoral characteristically presents a positive view of its world. This is not necessarily the case, as you will see later in this chapter. Poets have taken very similar subjects and presented them from strikingly different perspectives.

## The Pastoral and city life

There is a **sub-genre** known as 'urban pastoral', where the more positive views traditionally taken of the country are transferred to the city. In this context the urban working man may represent the simple, uncomplicated life often associated elsewhere with shepherds, and be used as a way to criticise the complex, even corrupt world of those operating at the top of the class structure.

However, the pastoral genre can also deal with city life in a more critical manner, contrasting it unfavourably with rural existence.

The following two poems take the city of London as their subject.

### Key terms

**Sub-genre:** a specific category within a less specific one. For example, the forensic crime novel is a sub-genre of crime fiction.

### Activity 3

Read the poems and, with a partner, identify the ways in which they present very different views. Try to come up with some ideas about the attitudes and values that underpin these two texts.

### Link

For a commentary on Activity 3, see the end of the chapter.

Earth has not anything to show more fair:
Dull would he be of soul who could pass by
A sight so touching in its majesty:

This city now doth, like a garment, wear
The beauty of the morning; silent, bare
Ships, towers, domes, theatres and temples lie
Open unto the fields and to the sky;
All bright and glistening in the smokeless air.
Never did sun more beautifully steep
In his first splendour, valley, rock or hill;
Ne'er saw I, never felt, a calm so deep!
The river glideth at his own sweet will:
Dear God! The very houses seem asleep;
And all that mighty heart is lying still!

***William Wordsworth***, Composed upon Westminster Bridge, *September 3, 1802*

I wander through each chartered street
Near where the chartered Thames does flow,
And mark in every face I meet
Marks of weakness, marks of woe.
In every cry of every man,
In every infant's cry of fear,
In every voice, in every ban,
The mind-formed manacles I hear:
How the chimney-sweeper's cry
Every black'ning church appals,
And the hapless soldier's sigh
Runs in blood down palace walls.
But most through midnight streets I hear
How the youthful harlot's curse
Blasts the new-born infant's tear
And blights with plague the marriage hearse.

***William Blake***, London, *1791*

### Link

For information on anti-pastoral, see later in this chapter, and Chapter 13.

## Pastoral characters

It is now worth looking at the operation of character within the pastoral genre.

### Link

For a commentary on Activity 4, see the end of the chapter.

### Activity 4

Read the following extract from the opening of Wordsworth's poem *The Pedlar* at least twice and make notes on the following question.

- In what ways does the character of the Pedlar fit in to your expectations of a pastoral character?

Him had I seen the day before, alone
And in the middle of the public way
Standing to rest himself. His eyes were turned
Towards the setting sun, while, with that staff
Behind him fixed, he propped a long white pack
Which crossed his shoulders, wares for maids who live
In lonely villages or straggling huts.
I knew him – he was born of lowly race
On Cumbrian hills, and I have seen the tear
Stand in his luminous eye when he described
The house in which his early youth was passed,
And found I was no stranger to the spot.
I loved to hear him talk of former days
And tell how when a child, ere yet of age
To be a shepherd, he had learned to read
His bible in a school that stood alone,
Sole building on a mountain's dreary edge,
Far from the sight of city spire, or sound
Of minster clock. From that bleak tenement
He many an evening to his distant home
In solitude returning saw the hills
Grow larger in the darkness, all alone
Beheld the stars come out above his head,
And travelled through the wood, no comrade near
To whom he might confess the things he saw.

***William Wordsworth**, The Pedlar, 1798*

Like the Pedlar, characters in pastoral writing are often representative of their community, and often, therefore, working men. This raises another question: Do you expect male or female characters to dominate pastoral writing? You will have the opportunity later to consider whether significantly different roles are allotted to men and women within the Pastoral.

### Activity 5

Find a significant character within your chosen pastoral text and decide to what extent he or she represents the traditional pastoral qualities or features you have encountered so far.

The figure of the Pedlar brings us back to the earlier association of the Pastoral with religion. The material you have read in this chapter should have suggested to you that there are many different ways of looking at the idea of the Pastoral. Here are some ideas for you to think about as you read the chapters that follow. You will have the opportunity to review these ideas towards the end of this unit.

1. Is there a basic contradiction between the simplicity of the pastoral vision and the often elaborate and sophisticated way in which it is presented in literature?
2. Here is an extract from Wordsworth's Preface to the *Lyrical Ballads*, 1800. The poet is defending his choice of subject matter. Do you find his ideas convincing?

   > Low and rustic life was generally chosen because in that situation the essential passions of the heart find a better soil in which they can attain their maturity, are under less restraint, and speak a plainer and more emphatic language.
3. Does the Pastoral basically engage in a game of make-believe? Is the world it depicts untrue to real life?
4. Is there at times a basic contradiction within the pastoral vision? If 'nature' is celebrated as something different from the artificial creations of humanity, does this take into account the degree to which the environment has been shaped, consciously and unconsciously, by human action? Is the relationship between 'art' and 'nature' therefore a very complex one?

### Extension activity

Research a literary map of Britain in which you identify and place writers familiar to you, particularly writers who have an important literary connection with the place where they were born or lived. Consider how many of these writers could be seen as operating within the pastoral tradition.

## What elements of the Pastoral have been identified so far?

- There is a close connection with rural life.
- Traditionally the Pastoral is associated with the life of shepherds.
- The view given of the countryside is usually, but not always, positive.
- Nostalgia for the past is an important component.
- There is a Christian aspect to the Pastoral.
- Traditional pastoral characters live a simple and isolated existence.

## Commentaries

### *Commentary on Activity 2*

The word 'nature' is not easily or simply defined. You will find a wide range of applications in the *Oxford English Dictionary*. In *Keywords: A Vocabulary of Culture and Society* (1983) the critic Raymond Williams made the famous comment, 'Nature is perhaps the most complex word in the language'. A distinction that many writers have made is between 'Nature' (a broad philosophical concept of a force that activates the world) and 'nature' (a collective term for the various earthly life forms). Do you think that humans are included within this definition of the term 'nature' or that it refers to what is non-human?

Your list may have included these phrases:

- good nature(d)
- human nature
- Mother Nature
- state of nature
- nature trail/study.

Even this limited list of phrases includes a range of references: to internal human qualities, to social practices (naturism/nudism), to terms for the external 'natural' world.

### Commentary on Activity 3

#### *Different views of London*

You will probably have decided that Wordsworth's poem offers a much more positive response to the London scene. A simple overview of the vocabulary of the poems will enable you to contrast 'majesty', 'beauty' and 'sweet' in the first with 'fear', 'curse', 'blights' and 'plague' in the second. Wordsworth's description of the city as being 'open unto the fields and to the sky' conveys a sense of freedom and space very different from the closed-in, oppressive view of the 'chartered street[s]' and 'chartered Thames' that we are presented with in Blake's poem.

This wider perspective operates from the opening line, and the opening reference to the 'Earth'. Although the concrete nouns of the sixth line refer to constructed, material things of the city, they are 'open unto the fields' and thus directly connected to the country, as would have been far more the case in the early 19th century. Line 10 gives a list of nouns that, apparently in contrast, refer to more geological and rural constructions, but the structure of the poem invites a sense of parallel with the earlier line.

*London* offers a list, a series of images that impress themselves on the consciousness of the narrator as he (?) wanders, apparently aimlessly, through the streets of the city. The first-person perspective is insistent, and adds to the anguished empathy of the speaker with the objects of his pity. The suffering of the inhabitants of the city is implicitly linked with the city buildings: church, palace walls and midnight streets. The personification here is very different in effect from the image of the city in the first poem wearing the beauty of the morning 'like a garment'. In addition, Wordsworth's poem seems to drift between third-, and first-person perspective, and humanity is, in comparison, absent.

#### *Language and structure*

You may also have connected with this differing emphasis other language features and structures within the poems. Wordsworth's exclamatory invocation in the last lines perhaps conveys some form of spiritual exultation, and the regular **iambic metre** and **sonnet** structure move the poem gracefully from a general survey of the scene to an expression of awe and admiration. Blake's language is simpler and more compressed; the heavy and insistent repetitions of the second verse reflect the dull and hopeless routines of the urban poor.

#### *Attitudes*

The attitudes of the two poets seem very different: in her journals, Wordsworth's sister, Dorothy, wrote of the same scene that 'there was even something like the purity of one of nature's own grand spectacles', and nature here for Wordsworth offers an opportunity to place the world

#### Key terms

**Iambic metre:** a verse pattern where metrical feet consist of an unstressed syllable followed by a stressed syllable.

**Sonnet:** a poem that usually consists of 14 lines in iambic metre, but has a considerable variety of rhyme schemes.

of man within a wider universe, and to link an appreciation of this natural universe with the growth of an individual consciousness. The landscape comes to provide an image of eternity and creative power: associated perhaps with the creative process itself.

For Blake, the immediate environment offers up images of tyranny, punitive law and corrupted church. Those things in life that are normally associated with creation and regeneration, love and children, are here blighted by the moral pollution that surrounds them. In fact, you might see this view as essentially **anti-pastoral**.

### Key terms

**Anti-pastoral:** a genre created to stand in opposition to the Pastoral, intended to subvert, to undermine the images and illusions on which the Pastoral is based.

### *Commentary on Activity 4*

This poem is Wordsworth's first sustained piece of autobiographical writing, but the narrative is largely in the third person, focusing on the story of the Pedlar.

The idea of the Pedlar living far from the busy life of towns or cities is one that you may have seen as characteristic of pastoral characters. The word 'alone' appears emphatically at the end of the opening line, and he is later associated with 'maids who live in lonely villages'. His school metaphorically represents the concept of isolation; it stands 'alone', the 'sole' building, significantly placed on the inaccessible 'dreary edge' of a mountain. From it, he returns home 'in solitude'.

You may also have anticipated the Pedlar's humble life; he grew up in a 'bleak tenement', and was 'born of lowly race'. Another significant aspect of the Pedlar's character is his connection with religion. We are told of his bible reading and he is associated with the idea of confession. There is however a sense that his religious feelings may not be conventionally Christian. He is physically distanced from the Christian symbols of spire and minster, but still carries a staff, the familiar property of the pilgrim.

The narrator seems to present the pedlar as a character to be admired; the pastoral world that he represents is thus also presented positively.

*Summary*

In this chapter introducing the Pastoral you have looked at a range of definitions and interpretations and have studied texts that reflect contrasting views of pastoral life. You have learnt that many elements of the Pastoral can be interpreted in very different and even apparently contradictory ways by different writers.

# 8 The Garden of Eden

*Aims of the chapter:*

- explores the significance of the Garden of Eden within the Pastoral
- looks at different ways in which gardens have been presented in pastoral literature.

The idea of the Garden of Eden lies at the heart of Western culture. The Garden offered a blissful state of paradise, from which Adam and Eve were banished because of their disobedience and sin. The paradise could only be regained for humanity through Christ's sacrifice on the Cross.

The significant place that gardens have long had in the lives of Europeans is in some ways connected with the desire to replicate some aspects of the beauty and innocence lost with the expulsion from Eden. Gardens have grown to be symbolic things in British culture; any survey of the media will quickly discover a bewildering range of magazines and television programmes devoted to gardening pursuits. Their importance lies in their dual function as places of either retreat and recreation or work and production (in some cases, of course, they can be both). The distinction between these two functions is often important in the Pastoral.

### Activity 1

**Make a list of phrases containing the word 'garden', including place names (e.g. Covent Garden) and divide them as far as you can into two categories: places of work and of recreation. See if the division suggests anything to you about the role of gardens in our society.**

### Link

For a commentary on Activity 1, see the end of the chapter.

## The expulsion from Eden

The disobedience of Adam and Eve, and their expulsion from Eden, is a story that carries within it many of the Pastoral's central concerns:

- Eden itself is seen as a place of rich and varied fertility.
- Within its boundaries lies an innocent world, which writers in later times often represented as confined to childhood.
- Its loss provides a model for a more general sense of regret for a lost and unattainable past.
- The apple that Adam and Eve eat symbolises both the goodness of nature and its perversion when put to corrupt use.
- The sexual knowledge gained by Adam and Eve comes at a price: the acknowledgement of the existence of sin and shame.
- Eden also contains within it a serpent, the means to its own destruction.
- After their departure from Eden, Adam and Eve become the first of a long list of literary wanderers in search of a home to replicate the one they have left behind.
- They are denied access to the Tree of Life and thus condemned to mortality. Time and death therefore become integral parts of human existence.

### Activity 2

**Read the following two accounts of the temptation and fall of Adam and Eve. Consider the second text in the context of its relationship to the first. Discuss with a partner what seem to you to be the significant differences between them. Look particularly at their narrative structures, the nature of their focus on the central characters, and the references to the tree.**

### Link

For a commentary on Activity 2, see the end of the chapter.

## Two accounts

The first account is from the King James Bible (1611).

### From the Book of Genesis

1 Now the serpent was more subtil than any beast of the field which the LORD God had made. And he said unto the woman, Yea, hath God said, Ye shall not eat of every tree of the garden?
2 And the woman said unto the serpent, We may eat of the fruit of the trees of the garden:
3 But of the fruit of the tree which is in the midst of the garden, God hath said, Ye shall not eat of it, neither shall ye touch it, lest ye die.
4 And the serpent said unto the woman, Ye shall not surely die:
5 For God doth know that in the day ye eat thereof, then your eyes shall be opened, and ye shall be as gods, knowing good and evil.
6 And when the woman saw that the tree was good for food, and that it was pleasant to the eyes, and a tree to be desired to make one wise, she took of the fruit thereof, and did eat, and gave also unto her husband with her: and he did eat.
7 And the eyes of them both were opened, and they knew that they were naked; and they sewed fig leaves together, and made themselves aprons.

*From Genesis Chapter 3*

The second account is from John Milton's *Paradise Lost* (1667). In this section of the poem, Satan, having entered into the body of the serpent, has begun his temptation of Eve, who has unwisely chosen to work apart from Adam. Eve has enquired how it is that a beast has gained the power of speech. (Note that you may need to look up the meanings of certain words here.)

To whom the guileful tempter thus replied:
'Empress of this fair World, resplendent Eve,
Easy to me it is to tell thee all
What thou command'st, and right thou shouldst be obeyed.
I was at first as other beasts that graze
The trodden herb, of abject thoughts and low,
As was my food, nor aught but food discerned
Or sex, and apprehended nothing high,
Till on a day, roving the field, I chanced
A goodly tree far distant to behold,
Loaden with fruit of fairest colours mixed,
Ruddy and gold: I nearer drew to gaze,
When from the boughs a savoury odour blown,
Grateful to appetite, more pleased my sense
Than smell of sweetest fennel, or the teats
Of ewe or goat dropping with milk at even,
Unsucked of lamb or kid, that tend their play.
To satisfy the sharp desire I had
Of tasting those fair apples, I resolved
Not to defer, hunger and thirst at once,
Powerful persuaders, quickened at the scent
Of that alluring fruit, urged me so keen. ...
Amid the tree now got, where plenty hung
Tempting so nigh, to pluck and eat my fill
I spared not, for such pleasure till that hour
At feed or fountain never had I found.

*Book IX, lines 567–88, 594–7*

### AQA Examiner's tip

In exploring important pastoral concepts, always remember to consider *how* the writers present their pastoral vision. Don't allow description of *content* to replace analysis of the writer's methods.

*Nicolas Poussin (1594–1665) developed a painting style that stressed the moral message of his compositions. In* The Arcadian Shepherds, *it is the shepherds who puzzle over the words 'Et in Arcadia ego'. Interestingly, an earlier version of the painting was at one time in the Duke of Devonshire's collection at Chatsworth, Derbyshire, one of the great English country estates.*

### Activity 3

Consider the degree to which temptation is a significant feature within your pastoral text.

## *Arcadia* and *Brideshead Revisited*

The central idea that within Eden lurks the force that may corrupt and destroy it, or destroy the possibility of the main characters continuing to inhabit that Eden, lies behind the phrase: 'Et in Arcadia ego'. Literally, this can be translated: 'I too dwell in Arcadia', and it is often used in the sense 'I also had my time in Arcadia' (i.e. experienced a time of blissful happiness). However, its appearance on a tomb in the picture 'The Arcadian Shepherds' by the 17th-century painter Nicolas Poussin suggests that it is death that lies in wait there. 'Et' can also mean 'even', and the translation 'Even in Arcadia, I am here' sounds a far more chilling note.

### Link

See 'The vocabulary of the Pastoral' in Chapter 7 for more on the meaning of Arcadia.

The following extract from Evelyn Waugh's novel *Brideshead Revisited* (1945) comes after the prologue, at the beginning of Chapter 1. The narrator, Charles Ryder, is an army officer during World War Two. He finds himself setting up a camp close to Brideshead, the family home of the Flyte family, with whom around twenty years previously his life became memorably entangled. The title of the first book, or section, of the novel is: 'Et in Arcadia Ego'.

### Activity 4

1. Read the passage and look at the ways in which both the countryside around Brideshead and Oxford University, where Charles is studying, are described.
2. What expectations do you have of this passage, bearing in mind what you know about the Pastoral?
3. Are there any ways in which these expectations are not met, and are there elements within the passage that you did not expect?

> 'I have been here before,' I said; I had been there before; first with Sebastian more than twenty years ago on a cloudless day in June, when the ditches were creamy with meadowsweet and the air heavy with all the scents of summer; it was a day of peculiar splendour, and though I had been there so often, in so many moods, it was to that first visit that my heart returned on this, my latest.
>
> That day, too, I had come not knowing my destination. It was Eights Week. Oxford – submerged now and obliterated, irrecoverable as Lyonesse, so quickly have the waters come flooding in – Oxford, in those days, was still a city of aquatint. In her spacious and quiet streets men walked and spoke as they had done in Newman's day; her autumnal mists, her grey springtime, and the rare glory of her summer days – such as that day – when the chestnut was in flower and the bells rang out high and clear over her gables and cupolas, exhaled the soft airs of centuries of youth.

***Evelyn Waugh***, Brideshead Revisited, *p23*

## Link

For a commentary on Activity 4, see the end of the chapter.

*Still from the television series of Brideshead Revisited*

## Corruption of the pastoral idyll

So where is the serpent in this novel? Is there any sense of the destructive, death-bringing 'I'?

It is arguable that the corruption of the pastoral idyll in *Brideshead Revisited* comes from within, whether within the flawed characters of the Flyte family or the institutions of the world of the novel. Betrayal, self-betrayal and remorseless decay destroy relationships and, symbolically, the great house itself.

The process begins early. The Oxford world of Charles and Sebastian is charming but adolescent, and when Sebastian's family begin to exercise increasing control over his behaviour, his rather pagan world takes on a very fragile air, and he vainly seeks escape.

> And since Sebastian counted among the intruders his own conscience and all claims of human affection, his days in Arcadia were numbered.

Brideshead Revisited, *p123*

*Brideshead Revisited* is a novel that is very much concerned with religion, and especially the Catholic faith. No main character is untouched by the effects of Catholicism during the narrative. In its concern with sin, and the need to acknowledge sin, the novel explores the pastoral world of the Garden of Eden at many levels.

## Did you know?

There is another pastoral idyll within the otherwise terrifying world of George Orwell's *1984*. Winston Smith, the central character, briefly escapes to what he calls the 'Golden Country', away from the brutal city of Big Brother.

## Activity 5

The extracts above have shown you how the pastoral vision of the Garden of Eden can be translated into more contemporary contexts. Eden can be presented under a different name, and its function within the narrative can be very varied.

- Is there a distinctive use of an image of Eden in your pastoral text?
- Do dreams play a part in its presentation?
- Does the vision of Eden operate within obviously political or religious contexts?

## Children's literature

The area of literature that is often designated 'Children's literature' has made wide use of the story of the Garden of Eden. One example is Lewis Carroll's *Alice's Adventures in Wonderland*. The garden in Wonderland is not altogether a comfortable fairy-tale place; there are many images of death and terror.

Another famous garden is that of Frances Hodgson Burnett's *The Secret Garden*. Here the garden has a more positive effect. The locked, abandoned garden is restored to life through the arrival of children who are themselves 'healed' by its influence.

A third example, much closer to the model of the original biblical tale, is *The Magician's Nephew*, by C.S. Lewis. This story has a more direct Christian theme, and it involves an apple, a boy and a girl who are tempted to disobey an order, and an offer of eternal life.

### Extension activities

**1 Children's literature**

Research the stories mentioned above, or any other examples of children's literature that you know which significantly involve a garden, and see to what extent and in what ways they deal with events or themes similar to those you have explored in this chapter.

**2 The symbol of the apple**

Explore the use that different writers make of the symbol of the apple, either in your own text or in other examples of the Pastoral. The eating of the apple can be seen to bring power or death; it can therefore represent good or evil. If it represents knowledge, can reason and knowledge sometimes be seen as evil? It is the focus of the temptation; the idea of forbidden fruit is a very potent one in our culture.

### Did you know?

The image of the garden as either a replica of the Garden of Eden or as a place for the pursuit of love was a strong element in medieval literature.

## Commentaries

### *Commentary on Activity 1*

Your list may have included such phrases as 'The Garden of England' and 'Welwyn Garden City' as well as 'Covent Garden'. All these use the word 'garden' to convey positive, rural associations, even within the boundaries of a city. This is not to say that 'Covent Garden' has no connections with the world of work. Its history marks an interesting progress from being an actual garden to becoming, by the late 16th century, the most famous market in England.

A 'garden centre' also overlaps the worlds of work and leisure, but perhaps phrases like 'garden party' and 'garden house' suggest the importance of gardens as retreats from the pressures of earning a living. The names of birds and butterflies such as the 'garden warbler' and the 'garden (common) white' testify to the significance of the garden as a habitat, and organisations like the RSPB place much emphasis on gardens as places where important conservation work may go on.

All this indicates how many-layered the **connotations** of the word 'garden' are in our culture. As indicated above, however, the most significant literary associations of the word continue to be in connection with the biblical Garden of Eden and the expulsion of Adam and Eve.

### Key terms

**Connotations:** the implications and associations of a word (rather than the directly represented meaning).

### *Commentary on Activity 2*

*Narrative structure*

You will have noticed that the first version is considerably more condensed. The complete story is told in a few paragraphs, whereas Milton devotes the whole of Book IX to an account of the temptation alone. You may also have commented on a shift in narrative focus. The events of the biblical version **foreground** God, both as an invisible presence and through the words attributed to him by the characters. In this extract from *Paradise Lost*, however, the focus of the narrative is on an ongoing debate between Satan and Eve. The opening line is characteristic of the way in which Book IX is structured through the use of **speech tags** which introduce the separate stages of the dialogue.

*Focus on characters*

There is also an interesting difference in the ways that the central characters are identified. In the biblical version Eve is only identified as 'the woman' (she is not actually named – significantly, by Adam – until verse 20, after the expulsion is confirmed). There is no direct indication that the serpent has been physically taken over by Satan. In contrast, in *Paradise Lost* the dramatic attention of the narrative is very much on the character and motivation of Satan.

The means whereby Satan seduces Eve constitute a central part of this section of *Paradise Lost*. His speech is an impressive display of debating skills, from the carefully chosen **invocation** 'Empress', to the deliberately structured argument that builds up to the crucial moment when he eats 'his fill', interestingly of fruit which hangs 'tempting' from the tree.

*References to the tree*

The tree itself occupies a central position in both narratives. In the biblical version it acts as the focus of the conversation between the serpent and 'the woman'. It is placed significantly 'in the midst of the garden' and the power of the fruit for good and evil is stressed: 'Ye shall not eat of it, neither shall ye touch it, lest ye die.' The appeal of the fruit is threefold: 'good for food', 'pleasant to the eyes' and having the power to 'make one wise'. Thus through the tree comes knowledge and therefore power; but the acquisition of power comes at a terrible price, bringing with it knowledge of sin, mortality and therefore death.

In *Paradise Lost*, Satan's opening words 'Empress', 'command'st' and 'obeyed' all foreground this idea of power, and the tree which will deliver this power is soon described as 'goodly'. Satan's developing description of the tree invokes classical pastoral images to convey its sensual appeal. The lines

> the teats
> Of ewe or goat dropping with milk at even,
> Unsucked of lamb or kid, that tend their play

are ironically built around images of innocence and life-enhancing nourishment drawn from a familiar earthly rural world. Here, then, a pastoral vision is deliberately evoked in the service of deception.

The tree is further associated with power through its height – above the reach of mere lowly beasts (but by implication not beyond Eve or Adam); the fruit is described as rich: 'loaden' and 'gold' in colour. Satan also, however, when describing the effect and nature of the tree, repeatedly uses words that stress the concept of temptation: 'alluring', 'urged me so keen', 'powerful persuaders', 'desire' and 'tempting'. Thus, while Satan is

#### Key terms

**Foreground:** in a piece of writing, to draw attention to something by means of a particular expression or use of language.

**Speech tags:** words like 'he replied', indicating the speaker and the nature of the speech act.

**Invocation:** an appeal, often to a higher power.

at pains to emphasise to Eve the irresistible appeal of the tree, the lines also convey to the reader the moral corruption that drives his argument.

### *Commentary on Activity 4*

You may have expected – and found – examples of rich evocative imagery, heavily dependent on sensual appeal, such as in the opening paragraph: 'creamy with meadowsweet', 'heavy with all the scents of summer'. There is also a familiar pastoral sense of an incomparable world and time: a 'cloudless day' of 'peculiar splendour'.

Ryder is looking back on a past which the novel will go on to show as irrecoverable. Oxford (or the Oxford of Charles Ryder and Sebastian Flyte) is described as a lost city, submerged by the metaphorical waters of time. The city is associated with 'centuries of youth', youth conventionally being a time of pastoral hope and innocence, but also inevitably subject to the decay that time will bring. The pastoral world, however, still offers a temporary escape from a less attractive wider world.

Oxford is also represented in terms that are as recognisably pastoral and sensual as those used in describing the countryside around Brideshead. The streets are 'quiet'; the autumn brings its 'mists', the summer its chestnut flowers and bells ringing out 'high and clear'. You might even feel that the **syntax** and rhythms of the narrative themselves convey the rich, slightly **elegiac** tone. The last sentence builds up through a succession of clauses to the climactic final phrase, slow and heavy with the soft **alliteration** of the 's' sound.

#### Key terms

**Elegiac:** from 'elegy', a lament for the dead, or for the loss of an idyllic state or experience.

**Alliteration:** the repetition, for effect, of consonants, especially at the beginnings of words.

You may also have noticed, but not expected, the focus of the insistently romantic effect of the passage. We are told, a few lines later, that Oxford has been invaded by 'a rabble of womanhood', from whom Charles and Sebastian have fled. This is emphatically, and almost exclusively, a world of young men, and much of the wistful longing is directed at past and lost male friendships.

### *Summary*

In this chapter you have explored the place of the Garden of Eden within the pastoral genre, as depicted in contrasting literary texts from the 17th century. You have looked at aspects of the pastoral idyll and its corruption in a modern novel and have applied what you have learnt to the pastoral text you are studying. You have also considered how gardens and the Garden of Eden are used in children's literature, and how writers have used the symbol of the apple.

# 9 Time and death in the Pastoral

*Aims of the chapter:*

- explores the importance of the elements of time and death in the Pastoral
- looks at some ways in which the seasons are presented in pastoral texts.

## Activity 1

1. List the months of the year and assign a colour to represent each one. Now do the same for the four seasons.
2. Consider the associations that the different colours have. Is it possible to see these colours, or the different times of the year, as an allegorical representation of the stages of human life?

Conventionally, spring represents new life and birth, the onset of autumn old age, and winter the approach of death. Did you find associations that offered a more complex picture? Spring, for instance, was a time of great hardship in agricultural societies, when the produce of the previous year's harvest was almost used up. Christian belief places a birth in the middle of winter and a death in spring.

Pastoral literature has frequently explored the concepts of time and death. The changing seasons of the year have offered writers an image of human birth, growth and ageing. Childhood has also been linked to the ideas of innocence that you have explored in relation to the Garden of Eden, and has offered writers an image of an irrecoverable, but much longed-for time, untainted by the knowledge of sin.

### Remember

**Elegiac** was defined in Chapter 8.

The elegiac tone of much pastoral writing is linked to this yearning for past joys. Ideas about the brevity of human life, and the sense that joys and pleasures can also be short-lived, have been expressed by pastoral writers through the imagery of vegetation: trees and flowers are inevitably and equally subject to the changes that time brings.

## Activity 2

Read carefully the following famous representation of a season, John Keats's ode *To Autumn*.

1. Focus on ideas about time and how these are represented within the poem.
2. Can you find any ways in which the poem deals with a wider sense of time than merely the season of autumn?
3. How is the idea of death explored here?

### Link

For a commentary on Activity 2, see the end of the chapter.

Autumn *by Giuseppe Arcimboldi (1527–93)*

I

Season of mists and mellow fruitfulness
Close bosom-friend of the maturing sun
Conspiring with him how to load and bless
With fruit the vines that round the thatch-eaves run;
To bend with apples the mossed cottage-trees,
And fill all fruit with ripeness to the core;
To swell the gourd and plump the hazel shells
With a sweet kernel; to set budding more
And still more, later flowers for the bees
Until they think warm days will never cease,
For summer has o'erbrimmed their clammy cells.

*II*

Who hath not seen thee oft amid thy store?
Sometimes whoever seeks abroad may find
Thee sitting careless on a granary floor,
Thy hair soft-lifted by the winnowing wind;
Or on a half-reaped furrow sound asleep,
Drowsed with fume of poppies, while thy hook
Spares the next swath and all its twined flowers:
And sometimes like a gleaner thou dost keep
Steady thy laden head across a brook;
Or by a cider-press, with patient look,
Thou watchest the last oozings hours by hours.

*III*

Where are the songs of Spring? Ay, where are they?
Think not of them, thou hast thy music too –
While barred clouds bloom the soft-dying day,
And touch the stubble-plains with rosy hue;
Then in a wailful choir the small gnats mourn
Among the river sallows, borne aloft
Or sinking as the light wind lives or dies;
And full-grown lambs loud bleat from hilly bourn:
Hedge-crickets sing; and now with treble soft
The redbreast whistles from a garden croft;
And gathering swallows twitter in the skies.

***John Keats**, To Autumn, 1819*

## AQA Examiner's tip

One of the Assessment Objectives (AO3) will require you to explore different interpretations of texts. This example shows one way of doing this. Note that you are not going to be asked which interpretation is 'right'! Note also that Jonathan Bate's analysis considers both the contexts of production (within what wider contexts the poem was produced) and reception (the contexts within which it might be read).

There is another, less comforting, way of reading this poem than that shown in the commentary on Activity 2. Jonathan Bate, in an essay entitled 'The Ode to Autumn as Ecosystem' (from *The Green Studies Reader*, 2000) has shown how the poem links time and space through its treatment of weather and also its incorporation of the sky, the hills and the cottage garden into a single unified world. But he also links the poem with the weather conditions prevailing at the time of its composition. In 1819, after three very poor years, there was a good summer followed by a rich and sunny autumn.

His further argument, however, is that our contemporary reading of the poem may be significantly affected by the fact that we live in a time of global warming, when the pattern of the seasons seems to be altering and we may no longer be confident that autumn and winter will conform to traditional expectations.

### Activity 3

What do you think of Jonathan Bate's reading of the poem? In the 21st century are we generally more uncomfortable about the likely impact of weather conditions on our future lives? Are you less able to respond to the text as a celebration of the predictable pattern of the seasons?

## Childhood

For many writers, memories of childhood are explored through descriptions of the places where their childhood was spent. As the days of childhood are lost and irrecoverable, so the landscape of childhood may also have been lost through agricultural or industrial development.

### Dylan Thomas and *Fern Hill*

Another famous poem that deals with ideas about childhood and time through a focus on a specific pastoral scene is *Fern Hill* by Dylan Thomas (1914–53). Written in the summer of 1945, it is based on memories of Fernhill, the farm run by his aunt, Ann Jones, where the young Dylan spent his summer holidays.

For the boy, the farm is a paradise, and one in which he can reign supreme: 'honoured among wagons I was prince of the apple towns'. It is a poem without other people; the boy is 'green and carefree' amongst barns, streams, stables and fields. If the farm is a sort of Eden, it is one where the boy has no companions apart from the animals and birds of the surrounding countryside. Within this self-centred world, however, time still asserts itself. Significantly, we are told that 'Time *let* me play', suggesting that this period of carefree innocence was always going to be brief, and could be enjoyed only as long as time permitted. In the second last stanza, the poet concedes:

> nothing I cared, at my sky blue trades, that time allows
> In all his tuneful turning so few and such morning songs
> Before the children green and golden
> Follow him out of grace

You may have noticed here the slight hint of menace behind the more conventionally positive images of the pastoral world. Time seems to be personified as a musician, 'tuneful turning', but one whose influence may be malevolent. The idea that children must inevitably follow him out of their world of 'grace' has echoes of the story of the Pied Piper.

### Activity 4

1. Read the last stanza of the poem below and discuss what seems to you to be important in terms of its treatment of time.
2. What seem to you to be the significant images at work here?
3. How does Thomas use colour in this stanza?

### Link

For a commentary on Activity 4, see the end of the chapter.

Nothing I cared, in the lamb white days, that time would take me
Up to the swallow thronged loft by the shadow of my hand,
In the moon that is always rising,
Nor that riding to sleep
I should hear him fly with the high fields
And wake to the farm forever fled from the childless land.
Oh as I was young and easy in the mercy of his means,
Time held me green and dying
Though I sang in my chains like the sea.

*From* ***Dylan Thomas,*** Fern Hill

### Did you know?

Dylan Thomas's short story *Peaches* is also based on the poet's memories of Fernhill. In the story the farm is called 'Gorsehill', and his aunt and uncle appear, not very heavily disguised, as the characters Uncle Jim and Aunt Annie. The narrator is a young boy whose excited immersion in the strange world of the farm is spoiled by the arrival of a friend and his disapproving mother.

### Activity 5

Look again at the extracts from Thomas's poem and then at your own pastoral texts. What evidence of the Pastoral's interest in time, the seasons and the human ageing process do you find in the texts you are studying?

### Activity 6

How are colours used in your pastoral texts? Is there any particular use made of the colour green?

## The seasons

You have seen how references to time in the pastoral genre can be both positive and negative. This also applies to the way that the seasons are presented. Conventionally, spring represents new growth or rebirth, but the texts you have read will have shown you that a more ambiguous response to the season is often possible. Even the pattern of seasonal change can provide a bitter reminder that human life does not allow for such regeneration.

R.S. Thomas's poem *A Peasant* (1946) considers the character of Iago Prytherch, who despite his name is 'an ordinary man'. He is presented to the reader in what are often deliberately unflattering terms. His mind is vacant, we are told, and his clothes are 'sour with years of sweat'. But the final lines (below) prevent us dismissing the character too easily. As a reader you may find yourself rethinking your earlier response and in some ways feeling rather inferior to Prytherch.

Yet this is your prototype, who, season by season
Against siege of rain and the wind's attrition,
Preserves his stock, an impregnable fortress
Not to be stormed even in death's confusion.
Remember him, then, for he, too, is a winner of wars,
Enduring like a tree under the curious stars.

*From* ***R.S. Thomas,*** A Peasant

### Link

For a commentary on Activity 7, see the end of the chapter.

### Activity 7

1. Which words from these final lines of *A Peasant* seem to you especially significant in shaping your response to the character?
2. How are references to the seasons used here?

### Activity 8

Look for examples in your pastoral texts where the seasons, or the weather conditions within the seasons, provide a challenge, something to be endured or triumphed over.

## Death

The season of winter is often used to represent death, and the pastoral vision often incorporates an acknowledgement of death as the end of all things. Death may come as the literal end of human life, or as a metaphorical reference to the passing of some idyllic period.

### *Brideshead Revisited*

Evelyn Waugh's *Brideshead Revisited* chronicles the fall of the Marchmain family. The novel is structured around a series of deaths: the death of love, the death of individuals, the death of a civilisation. Many of the characters lapse into a sort of sterility: there is little indication at the end of the novel that the Marchmain line will continue. What does survive is religious faith. It is the Catholic religion that Waugh portrays as triumphing over death.

### Remember

Earlier in this chapter you were re-introduced to the term 'elegy'. The elegy mourns the loss of an idyllic state or experience and is a familiar pastoral form. Some elegies express the sad belief that what is lost can never be recovered.

### Link

See Chapter 8 for more on *Brideshead Revisited*, especially the section 'Et in Arcadia Ego'.

### Activity 9

1. Read the following extracts from *Brideshead Revisited* and consider the sorts of 'death' and attitudes to death that are presented.
2. Consider also the narrative methods used and how far they are like the techniques you have seen so far in your study of the pastoral genre.

There is no commentary on this activity.

### *Extract 1*

This extract comes at the end of the section 'Et in Arcadia Ego'. Sebastian Flyte, the second son of Lord Marchmain, is about to be sent down from Oxford. The carefree, **hedonistic** period of his youth, and that of the narrator, Charles Ryder, is about to come to an end.

### Key terms

**Hedonistic:** choosing to follow a life of pleasure.

**1 From 'Et in Arcadia Ego'**

But the shadows were closing round Sebastian. We returned to Oxford and once again the gillyflowers bloomed under my windows and the chestnut lit the streets and the warm stones strewed their flakes upon the cobble; but it was not as it had been; there was mid-winter in Sebastian's heart.

*p135*

### *Extract 2*

Here, at the end of the novel, Charles Ryder reflects on the gradual decay of the great house. After this paragraph, however, Charles sees the workings of providence, the lasting evidence of God's power, in the fact that the chapel has survived, and the light 'burned once more before the altar'.

**2 From the end of the novel**

The builders did not know the uses to which their work would descend; they made a new house with the stories of the old castle; year by year the great harvest of timber in the park grew to ripeness; until, in sudden frost came the age of Hooper; the place was desolate and the work all brought to nothing; Quomodo sedet sola civitas. Vanity of vanities, all is vanity.

*p331*

## Hint

1. Hooper is a young officer in Ryder's company. He is an unromantic, unsophisticated representative of the 'common man' of the new age.
2. 'Quomodo sedet sola civitas' is a Latin phrase meaning 'how solitary the city sits'.
3. 'Vanity of vanities, all is vanity' comes from Ecclesiastes 1:2. It refers to the inevitable destruction that time brings, and the foolishness of placing too much value on earthly things.

## Commentaries

### *Commentary on Activity 2*

You may have found an increasingly elegiac tone in this poem. There is a clear progression through the stanzas, particularly in terms of time. The opening verse has an eye on the recently departed summer and seems to be set in the middle of the day. The second stanza concerns itself with the gathering of the harvest celebrated in stanza one; the last line, with its reference to 'last oozings', suggests a further passing of time. The third verse is full of the vocabulary of maturity and even death: 'soft-dying day', 'mourn', 'wailful choir' and the wind that 'lives or dies'. Winter is approaching and spring seems far away.

So the structure of the poem, carefully developed and interwoven, creates its own unity, a unity that is tied to the familiar pattern and unity of the changing seasons. 'If winter comes can spring be far behind?' goes the proverbial saying. The pastoral vision acknowledges the passing of time and the inevitability of death for all living things, but life itself continues: the last verse, with its references to swallows and lambs, already looks forward to the next spring.

### *Commentary on Activity 4*

You may have commented on the way that time is again personified as an all-powerful figure that will lead the child out of its innocent world. Ideas of sleep and waking accompany this sense of loss of paradise. The reference to singing conveys the child's delighted response to life, but the image of the sea, with its moon-controlled ebb and flow, is not altogether reassuring.

'Lamb white' here conveys a sense of youth and innocence, not unlike the earlier effect of 'sky blue'. The impact of 'green' is more ambiguous. 'Green' is a central colour in the pastoral experience, but Thomas seems to use it in a distinctive way in this stanza. In the previous stanza, 'green' was linked with 'golden' to describe the boy and children in general, perhaps combining an idea of innocence with that of being somehow especially privileged. However, in the second last line of the poem we have 'green and dying'. Here the conventionally positive associations of green have been subverted. 'Green' here links with decay and mould; death hovers behind the child's world.

### *Commentary on Activity 7*

You may have selected some of these words:

- 'prototype': in one sense this could confirm the impression of Prytherch as a rather primitive creature; on the other it could suggest that he is an original, from whom those who follow are merely copies.
- 'stock': this could refer to his animals or his descendants.

- 'impregnable fortress': these words, together with others in the following lines, convey a sense of rugged military defiance, an instinct for survival against the odds.
- 'Remember him': this imperative phrase suggests that there are important lessons to be learned about the significance of his life.

You may also have noticed how Iago Prytherch is defined in terms of his ability to last out the seasons. They are the hostile forces that he endures, 'enduring like a tree'. The pastoral simile allies him with the world of nature; this too must endure the changing seasons.

### Hint

An **imperative** phrase is one that gives an instruction or order.

*Summary*

In this chapter you have explored the subjects of time and death in a range of pastoral texts. You have seen that the past is often evoked through reminiscences of childhood, which is often presented as a time of innocence. Death, though, is also acknowledged in the Pastoral, and frequently linked to the changing seasons of the year.

# 10 Journeys in the Pastoral

*Aims of the chapter:*

- considers the importance of journeys in pastoral texts
- looks at the ways in which journeys operate within the narrative structure
- compares and contrasts two pastoral texts.

Many of the texts you have read so far have involved the idea of a journey. In the previous chapter you looked at the importance of time within the pastoral genre. The concept of time itself involves the idea of a journey, of (possibly) linear progression, of movement. The idea of movement is integral to the Pastoral in many ways and is often presented in the form of a physical journey.

## Analysing narrative methods and structures

Remember what you learned about narrative methods in Unit 1. The distinction between story and plot is very important. The story may be thought of as the chronological order of events, and the plot as the chain of causes and circumstances that connect the various events and place them into some sort of relationship with each other.

There are many ways in which you might analyse how the narrative in your text is shaped.

### Contrasts

Some theorists have focused on the idea of opposites as a means of exploring narrative structures. In the pastoral genre this might involve contrasts between country and city, male and female, past and present, young and old – or, in relation to a journey, home and away.

### Did you know?

The word 'picaresque' comes from the Spanish 'picaro', meaning a rogue.

### The picaresque

The type of story called 'picaresque' is a familiar form of pastoral narrative. Picaresque plot usually involves the journey of a disreputable servant and his master, during which a series of adventures or misfortunes happen to them.

### Retreat and return

Terry Gifford in his book *Pastoral* (1999) focuses on the narrative pattern of retreat and return.

- The *retreat* may be from the court, the city, or the present.
- The *return* characteristically occurs after some insight or knowledge has been gained.
- Both of these, clearly, suggest a journey.

All of these above approaches can lend themselves to the exploration of the concept of the journey within the pastoral genre. Further reference will be made to them during this chapter.

### Activity 1

**Discuss which of these methods of exploring narrative patterns seem to you most useful when exploring your own pastoral texts.**

The film genre of the American Western includes many features of the Pastoral. The relationship, for instance, of (usually) man and his environment is often very important. There is often a contrast between the comparatively civilised world of the townships and the cowboy's life on the prairie.

### Activity 2

Collect together some examples of the Western and explore their use of a journey as a plot device.

## Two pastoral texts: *The Adventures of Huckleberry Finn* and *The Wind in the Willows*

At first sight these two texts might seem very dissimilar, so much so that little meaningful comparison is possible between them.

*Huckleberry Finn*, by Mark Twain, is set in America, in the Mississippi country, towards the end of the 19th century. It tells the tale of the voyage of a boy, Huck, and Jim, a runaway slave down the Mississippi, each in search of a different form of freedom.

*The Wind in the Willows*, by Kenneth Grahame, written in 1908, is firmly set in Edwardian England. It is often thought of as a children's book and records the adventures of four riverside animals. The action is largely, but not wholly, confined to the countryside where they live.

Some points of contact may already have suggested themselves to you.

- Both texts are connected with youth and the world of children.
- Both base their story around a river.
- Both, from the point of view of a modern reader, are set in the past.

A contrast and comparison of these two texts, therefore, may suggest some ways in which you can explore the importance of the idea of a journey in pastoral texts.

### Beginnings and endings

Two significant features of most fictional journeys are their beginning and their ending.

1 What motive impels the characters on their journey in the first place?
2 What, if anything, have the characters learnt by the end of their journey?

#### *Beginnings*

*Huckleberry Finn*

*Huckleberry Finn* begins with Huck positioning himself as a character strangely caught between the worlds of fact and fiction.

> You don't know about me, without you have read a book by the name of 'The Adventures of Tom Sawyer', but that ain't no matter. That book was made by Mr Mark Twain, and he told the truth, mainly.

The Adventures of Huckleberry Finn, *p49*

Huck's individual narrative voice and independent spirit will dominate the novel. He finds himself obliged to flee the **matriarchal** society of St Petersburgh, well represented by 'the widow', with whom he lives, and her sister, the sharp-tongued Miss Watson.

### Key terms

**Matriarchal:** where a mother (or mother figure) acts as the head of the family or social group.

A more urgent problem for Huck, however, is the sudden reappearance of his violent and drunken father. So Huck fakes his own murder and takes off in a canoe. Shortly into his journey he meets up with the runaway slave, Jim, who has his own urgent reasons for escape.

For Huck, even on the first night of his travels, the Mississippi River is both a consolation and a companion:

> When it was dark I set by my camp fire smoking, and feeling pretty satisfied; but by-and-by it got sort of lonesome, and so I went and set on the bank and listened to the currents washing along, and counted the stars and drift-logs and rafts that come down, and then went to bed; there ain't no better way to put in time when you are lonesome; you can't stay so, you soon get over it.

*p91*

The island on which Huck has temporarily landed, and where he meets Jim, also comes to represent his new-found freedom. The use of the first-person pronoun and stress on the words 'boss', 'belonged' and 'know' indicate a sense of possession, sharply different from the world Huck has left behind, where he owned next to nothing.

> But the next day I went exploring around down through the island. I was boss of it; it all belonged to me, so to say, and I wanted to know all about it.

*p92*

Crucially, though, the river provides a means of physical escape. Here, Huck's knowledge and understanding of the world of the river is crucially important to his survival.

> I shot past the head at a ripping rate, the current was so swift, and then I got into the dead water and landed on the side towards the Illinois shore. I run the canoe into a deep dent in the bank that I knowed about: I had to part the willow branches to get in; and when I made fast nobody could a seen the canoe from the outside.

*p88*

Twain presents Huck as someone wholly in tune with his environment; one of the many ways in which he is revealed as a 'natural' being, as opposed to the corrupted citizens of 'civilisation'. In the above passage Huck almost seems to absorb himself into the bankside vegetation; the world of nature shelters and protects him.

## Activity 3

Read the following extracts from *The Wind in the Willows* and consider the ways in which the presentation of the journey at the beginning of this story compares and contrasts with *Huckleberry Finn*. You might compare:

- the nature of the narrative voice
- the motivation for the journey
- the appeal of the river
- any other points that you think are important.

### Link

For a commentary on Activity 3, see the end of the chapter.

### *The Wind in the Willows*

The mole 'had been working hard all morning' and decides to abandon the boring task of underground spring-cleaning. He wanders happily off through the meadows until he finds himself on the bank of the river.

> He thought his happiness was complete when, as he meandered aimlessly along, suddenly he stood by the edge of a full-fed river. Never in his life had he seen a river before – this sleek, sinuous, full-bodied animal, chasing and chuckling, gripping things with a gurgle and leaving them with a laugh, to fling itself on fresh playmates that shook themselves free, and were caught and held again.

The Wind in the Willows, *p4*

The mole then meets the rat who swiftly initiates him into riverside life. He extols the virtues of living by a river.

> 'It's my world, and I don't want any other. What it hasn't got is not worth having, and what it doesn't know is not worth knowing. Lord! The times we've had together! Whether in winter or summer, spring or autumn, it's always got its fun and excitements.'

*p7*

**AQA Examiner's tip**

Remember that you will be required to show understanding of the ways in which writers use language. Identifying the nature of the narrative voice is a very important part of this process.

### *Endings*

The ending of *Huckleberry Finn* has provoked a great deal of critical controversy. The last chapters are taken over by the character of Tom Sawyer as he and Huck construct an elaborate fiction to 'free' Jim from slavery, when unknown to Jim and Huck he has already been given his freedom in Miss Watson's will.

Nevertheless, there remains the question of what Huck has learnt. It could be argued that Huck has learnt relatively little; he is still frequently puzzled by the complexities of the social world in which he finds himself. The Phelps' farm in Arkansas, where the story ends, is very much like the society of St Petersburgh, where it begins. But this resolution, this 'return' after the pastoral retreat, offers Huck little satisfaction. Where he does find hope is in another journey, another flight, as the last words of the story show.

> But I reckon I got to light out for the Territory ahead of the rest, because Aunt Sally she's going to adopt me and sivilize me and I can't stand it. I been there before.

Huckleberry Finn, *p369*

**Hint**

Aunt Sally is Tom Sawyer's aunt. The 'Territory' was at that time an Indian Reservation, also the haunt of fugitives from justice.

*The Wind in the Willows* ends with a less problematic restoration of the harmony that existed at the beginning of the story. Toad is restored to his stately home; the usurping stoats and weasels have been vanquished, and the world of the river bank resumes its tranquil existence.

> After this climax, the four animals continued to lead their lives, so rudely broken in upon by civil war, in great joy and contentment, undisturbed by further risings or invasions. ... Sometimes, in the course of long summer evenings, the friends would take a stroll together in the Wild Wood, now successfully tamed so far as they were concerned; and it was pleasant to see how respectfully they were greeted by the inhabitants.

The Wind in the Willows, *p157*

### Link

For a commentary on Activity 4, see opposite.

### Activity 4

Read the above passage from *The Wind in the Willows* carefully. Does the vocabulary used suggest any wider context within which the text might be read?

Many critics have commented on the social and political issues raised by the story. The ending, for instance, effectively re-establishes the status quo; the original social order has been restored after a period of radical upheaval, and the revolutionary elements have been safely subdued. In this reading, the stoats, weasels and ferrets represent the increasingly politically conscious working classes of the late 19th century, and Mole, Rat, Badger and Toad stand, in different ways, for members of the propertied middle or upper-middle classes. The period when Grahame wrote *The Wind in the Willows* was one of considerable simmering social discontent, and there is biographical evidence to suggest that Grahame was uneasy at the implications of these political developments.

This is a political reading of the ending of the story. From another perspective, the ending might suggest that Arcadia has been restored and that a satisfactorily 'pastoral' conclusion has been achieved. Toad, after all, can be argued to have learnt the error of his ways. The other animals prevent him carrying out his plan to use the victory banquet as a stage for his boastful speeches and songs, and for once in his life he agrees to keep a low profile:

> There were some knockings on the tables and cries of 'Toad! Speech! Speech from Toad! Song! Mr Toad's song!' But Toad only shook his head gently ...
>
> He was indeed an altered Toad!

The Wind in the Willows, *p156*

### Activity 5

Consider the ending of one of your pastoral texts.

- Is there any sense that the end of a journey has brought increased understanding?
- Has there been an internal journey to parallel the external one?

When considering the structure of *Huckleberry Finn* and *The Wind in the Willows* or any other pastoral text, you may find these literary terms useful:

- **Allegory:** a narrative that can be read on more than one level (perhaps a surface meaning and a meaning under the surface – like a fable).
- **Epic:** a long narrative – often a poem – on a heroic scale, dealing with great deeds, dangerous journeys and outsize characters. Tolkien's *The Lord of the Rings* is an example of an epic.
- **Myth:** a complex term, usually referring to a story that is not 'true' and deals with the supernatural and ideas of creation.

### Extension activities

1. Take any two fictional journeys that you know and exchange the settings (for example, with the texts above move *The Wind in the Willows* to America and *Huckleberry Finn* to England). In what ways would this affect the narratives?
2. Look at some other examples of 'children's' literature in the pastoral genre (for example *Alice's Adventures in Wonderland*) where a significant journey is involved. In what ways does the central character return from the journey with greater knowledge?

## Commentaries

### *Commentary on Activity 3*

A significant difference between the two narrative voices is that the first-person narrative of *Huckleberry Finn* does not feature in *The Wind in the Willows*. Huck's non-standard dialect and idiolect (speech characteristic of a specific individual) help to establish him as an honest narrator, one unlikely to deliberately mislead the reader. The third-person narrative of *The Wind in the Willows*, however, also conveys an individual point of view, in the case of the first extract that of the Mole.

Like Huck, the Mole is motivated to travel through a need to escape, but here the escape is from boredom. In a sense, this fits in with Terry Gifford's view of retreat and return: the retreat is from the restrictions of the everyday world.

The river, in both stories, is a place of power and beauty. Its continual movement creates a sense of freedom. Its endless variety contrasts with the routines of the worlds Huck and the Mole have left behind. The range of delights it offers is linked by the Rat to the changing seasons. Significantly, the Mole sees it as having the characteristics of another animal. Understandably there is less of a sense of real danger in the river of *The Wind in the Willows*. Words like 'chasing and chuckling' in the first extract establish the idea of carefree play. The threat of death is seldom far from the river of *Huckleberry Finn*.

### *Commentary on Activity 4*

You may have noticed such words and phrases as 'rudely broken in upon', 'civil war', 'risings or invasions', 'successfully tamed' and 'respectfully'. These suggest that, on one level, the story is about power and authority.

*Summary*

In this chapter you have learnt that many pastoral stories involve the idea of a journey. This journey can be both external (the characters travel a significant distance) and internal (the characters come to learn something about themselves and their world). You have explored the beginnings and endings of the journeys in two contrasting pastoral texts.

# 11 Pastoral love and romance

*Aims of the chapter:*

- looks at how pastoral writing explores love and marriage
- studies the use of natural imagery in pastoral texts
- explores the role of women in pastoral literature
- considers aspects of narrative method and the significance of context.

In the next chapter you will be exploring pastoral drama, and in particular comic drama. One of the main elements of comedy is the comic resolution of marriage. Love and marriage are central concerns of pastoral writing, and not merely in dramatic form.

## The use of natural imagery

A familiar literary convention is to explore the pleasures and pains of love through the use of natural imagery. Consider, for instance, the poetic image of the rose.

### Activity 1

Why do you think the rose has been such a popular symbol of love?

### Link

For a commentary on Activity 1, see the end of the chapter.

A famous poem that uses the image of the rose to represent love is Robert Burns's *A Red, Red Rose*. Literary historians and the tourist industry have frequently portrayed Burns both as an energetic lover and as a love poet, in some ways doing an injustice to his more complex achievements. Nevertheless, there is no doubt that he created some of the most memorable love songs in our culture.

### Activity 2

Look at the opening verse of Burns's poem. How is the image of the rose used within the verse?

### Link

For a commentary on Activity 2, see the end of the chapter.

O, my love is like a red, red rose
That's newly sprung in June.
O, my love is like a melody,
That's sweetly played in tune.

*From* **Robert Burns**, A Red, Red Rose, *1794*

### Activity 3

Read the following traditional ballad, *Let No Man Steal Your Thyme*, and consider the use made of pastoral imagery.

How are the images of trees and plants used to represent a woman's vulnerability?

Come all you fair and tender girls
That flourish in your prime,
Beware, beware, keep your garden fair,
Let no man steal your thyme.

For when your thyme is past and gone
He'll care no more for you
And in the place where your thyme was waste
Will spread all o'er with rue.

For woman is a branchy tree
And man's a clinging vine;
And from her branches carelessly
He'll take what he can find.

Let No Man Steal Your Thyme

### *Commentary on Activity 3*

There are at least five images worth exploring here:

1 thyme
2 rue
3 the garden
4 the tree
5 the vine.

Here is a short explanation of each image:

1 Thyme is a fragrant herb, commonly used in cooking. Its use here seems to be to represent a woman's virginity, the loss of which in earlier societies would drastically affect not only her reputation, but also her value as a potential wife. The **homophone** time/thyme is also important: the loss of her 'time' could suggest her time as a maiden, once lost never recovered.
2 Rue is an evergreen shrub whose leaves have a bitter taste. In this ballad it represents the bitter regret that a woman may feel after she has given herself to a faithless lover.
3 The 'garden fair' may here represent the wider sense of the woman's world, her life which needs to be carefully looked after.
4 The image of a tree portrays the woman as a firm, independent being, with a sort of richness represented by her branches.
5 The vine stands for the parasitic and predatory man, taking advantage of the woman.

In addition, you might consider the use of the words 'fair and tender' and 'flourish' to describe the girls. These words also have associations with the pastoral world of crops and flowers. The ballad form, with its simple language, its focus on a particular incident, and its strongly narrative method, was a popular means of storytelling in past rural societies.

#### Key terms

**Homophone:** a word sounding the same as another word but spelt differently.

## The role of women in pastoral literature

The role of women in ballads, and in other forms of pastoral literature, is very significant in terms of the treatment of love within this genre.

Kate Soper, in her book *What is Nature?* (1995), explores the portrayal of women in nature writing. Amongst others, she makes these points:

- The female, because of her role in child-bearing, has traditionally been associated with the body rather than the mind in the mind/body division. This connection has led to the further association of women and nature.
- In literature, nature is often represented as 'female' (e.g. 'Mother Nature', or such classical deities as Ceres).
- Landscape is often viewed as female, the land being seen as womb-like, as the source of life.
- There is a further analogy in society's exploitation and domination of the land and women.
- After women and/or nature have been 'mastered', there can follow a sense of regret for what has been defiled. (The word 'deflowered' has an interesting double reference here.)

### Did you know?

Ceres is the Roman goddess of agriculture – the harvest of the earth.

### Group activity

1. Are women significantly associated with nature within the pastoral world of your texts?
2. Make some careful selections that illustrate the presentation of women, or the use of imagery that connects women with the world of nature, and consider their effects within the text that you are studying.

### AQA Examiner's tip

You need to explore context (AO4) in your reading. Your study of the Pastoral will have shown you the significance of the contexts in which the pastoral texts were composed. Your readings may challenge contemporary perspectives. Attitudes to women, for instance, may well have altered significantly. In this way you will learn how the context of reception may also influence interpretation.

*Ceres, the Roman goddess of agriculture*

Famously, Ophelia in Shakespeare's *Hamlet* uses the language of flowers to express her anguished thoughts during her later madness. Each flower she selects and passes to other characters in the play carries a message:

> (*To the King*) There's fennel for you, and columbines – (*To the Queen*) There's rue for you, and here's some for me – we may call it herb of grace o'Sundays – O, you must wear your rue with a difference – There's a daisy ...'

Hamlet *4.5, 175–8*

Here, for instance, fennel stands for flattery – very appropriate for a king to receive. The ballad you read earlier in this chapter mentioned rue – often linked with sorrow. The daisy traditionally represented falsehood in love.

## *Tess of the d'Urbervilles*

Thomas Hardy's *Tess of the d'Urbervilles* (1891) is another example of a text which illustrates the idea that the exploitation of women can be expressed through pastoral imagery.

The early seduction or rape of Tess by her supposed relative, Alec d'Urberville, has left her alone and the bearer of a guilty secret. During the course of the novel, Tess is manipulated and betrayed by a series of men, leading to her final and tragic fate.

In the following extract, Tess has been attracted by the sound of the harp-playing of Angel Clare, a well-educated young man who has recently arrived to work at the same dairy farm as Tess. The two young people have begun to feel an attraction to each other.

> The outskirt of the garden in which Tess found herself had been left uncultivated for some years, and was now damp and rank with juicy grass which sent up mists of pollen at a touch; and with tall blooming weeds emitting offensive smells – weeds whose red and yellow and purple hues formed a polychrome as dazzling as that of cultivated flowers. She went stealthily as a cat through this profusion of growth, gathering cuckoo-spittle on her skirts, cracking snails that were underfoot, staining her hands with thistle-milk and slug-slime, and rubbing off upon her naked arms sticky blights which, though snow-white on the apple-tree trunks, made madder stains on her skin; thus she drew quite near to Clare, still unobserved of him.

***Thomas Hardy***, Tess of the d'Urbervilles, *pp178–9*

### Activity 4

**How are the details of the scene in this extract used to convey feeling and sensation?**

### Link

For a commentary on Activity 4, see the end of the chapter.

In the following chapter, Angel Clare's increasing infatuation is signalled to us by his playfully addressing Tess by the names of classical (and pastoral) goddesses. (This also indicates Clare's rather self-indulgent tendency to idealise Tess. His failure to appreciate her as a real, flawed, flesh-and-blood human being is to have disastrous consequences.)

# 12 Pastoral drama

*Aims of the chapter:*

- explores the pastoral elements of dramatic comedies, with particular reference to *As You Like It* and *She Stoops to Conquer*
- considers the use of setting in pastoral drama
- examines the relationship between pastoral elements and dramatic structure.

## Dramatic comedies

In 2005 the nature writer Richard Mabey published a book called *Nature Cure*, in which he gave an account of his recovery from depression, and the significant part that the natural world played in that recovery.

Towards the end of the book, Mabey considers the essential qualities of nature itself. He argues that the way the natural world operates is essentially comic, being about 'durability, survival, reconciliation'.

These are also the usual qualities of **dramatic comedies**.

- The characters of comedy operate within a clear social environment. Some of these characters are 'victims' within the plot. They tend in one way or another to be out of sympathy with their community; they have to be mocked into conformity.
- The heroes and heroines of comedy survive because of their ability to withstand the tests and traps that life sets them.
- The endings of comedy are crucially about achieving reconciliation. There will often be exceptions, those who cannot be absorbed into the world of their fellow citizens, but comedies traditionally end with the celebratory festival of marriage.
- Thus, in contrast to the final death toll of tragedies, comedies conclude with the triumph of love and the (theoretic) promise of regeneration through the children who may emerge from the characters' marriages.

Thus the workings of comedy can be paralleled to the processes of the natural world; the essential purpose of both is to preserve and increase life in all its forms. Those life forms which, like the classic comic protagonist, adapt and accommodate themselves to circumstances, will survive. Note also that it is tragic characters who often find themselves unable to bend with the prevailing winds of fate.

It is unsurprising, then, that pastoral elements play such an important part in dramatic comedies.

### Activity 1

Choose a central character from any pastoral play that you are studying and apply some of the criteria indicated above. To what extent do they fit in with how you see the personality and role of the character you have chosen?

### *As You Like It*

Shakespeare's *As You Like It* is a famous example of a play with many of the features generally associated with the pastoral genre. Below is a list of the characters in the play.

### Key terms

**Dramatic comedy:** a play whose plot moves towards a generally happy conclusion, often involving the unravelling of a complex romantic entanglement. Comic characters tend to be of fairly humble social background (compared with those of tragedy). Comedies may be expected to provoke laughter, but the degree to which this forms the main purpose of the drama will vary considerably from play to play.

### AQA Examiner's tip

Drama, itself a genre, has its own methods and conventions. When exploring drama texts make sure that you treat the texts as drama, plays written for performance, and not as though they were novels or biographies.

### Activity 2

Read through with a partner the list below of the characters in *As You Like It*.

1. Which characters from the list seem to you to be typically 'pastoral'?
2. Divide the characters into two groups on the basis of the pastoral distinction between court and country.
3. Do any two or more of these characters seem likely to have a connection that may be significant within the plot?
4. What do the names of some of the characters tell you about their function in the play?

### Link

For a commentary on Activity 2, see the end of the chapter.

Duke Senior, *a banished duke*
Amiens and Jaques, *noblemen in attendance on him*
Duke Frederick, *his brother, the usurper*
Le Beau, *a courtier*
Charles, *a wrestler*
Olivier, Jaques, Orlando, *sons of Sir Rowland de Boys*
Adam, Dennis, *servants of Olivier*
The Clown, *alias Touchstone*
Sir Oliver Martext, *a country vicar*
Corin, Silvius, *shepherds*
William, *a country youth, in love with Audrey*
Rosalind, *daughter of Duke Senior, later disguised as Ganymede*
Celia, *daughter of Duke Frederick, later disguised as Aliena*
Phebe, *a shepherdess*
Audrey, *a country wench*
A masquer representing Hymen
Lords, pages and attendants

### Did you know?

Hymen is the god of marriage in both Greek and Roman mythology.

### Activity 3

Try out the same process with any other play you are reading. *The Winter's Tale*, for instance, divides up its characters very much on court/country lines.

## *She Stoops to Conquer*

Oliver Goldsmith's comedy *She Stoops to Conquer* (1773) is another play where the worlds of town and country collide. The opening lines of the play establish this collision through the opposing views of Mrs and Mr Hardcastle.

> *Scene: A Chamber in an old fashioned House*
>
> *Enter* Mrs Hardcastle *and* Mr Hardcastle
>
> ***Mrs Hardcastle:*** I vow, Mr Hardcastle, you're very particular. Is there not a creature in the whole country, but ourselves, that does not take a trip to town now and then, to rub off the rust a little? There's the two Miss Hoggs, and our neighbour, Mrs Grigsby, go to take a month's polishing every winter.
>
> ***Hardcastle:*** Ay, and bring back vanity and affectation to last them the whole year. I wonder why London cannot keep its own fools at home? In my time, the follies of the town crept slowly among us, but now they travel faster than a stagecoach. Its fopperies come down, not only as inside passengers, but in the very basket.

***Oliver Goldsmith***, She Stoops to Conquer, *from Act 1 Scene 1*

### Activity 4

1. How does this opening to the play establish the town/country opposition?
2. What qualities of the town and country are claimed by the two characters?

### Link

For a commentary on Activity 4, see the end of the chapter.

The distaste for the country that Mrs Hardcastle indicates is to a certain extent also demonstrated by Marlow, whose romance with Hardcastle's daughter Kate provides the central plot of the play. He arrives from town as a rather reluctant suitor for her hand, and is further irritated by what he sees as the inconveniences of country life.

> 'What a tedious uncomfortable day have we had of it! We were told it was but forty miles across the country, and we have come above threescore.'

*From Act 1 Scene 2*

(Much of the following action, however, exposes Marlow's assumptions of superiority to some fairly painful examination. He finds himself continually baffled and outwitted by the local characters. These country characters prove less simple and one-dimensional than he imagines.)

### Activity 5

Consider the characters in any pastoral play that you are reading.

1. What qualities are attributed to those from the town and to those from the country?
2. Are stereotypical views (that is, the typical presumptions made about town and country people) in any way challenged by the play?

## The use of setting in pastoral drama

The significance of the pastoral setting in plays such as those mentioned above extends to more than providing a simple stage on which the action takes place. The setting is likely to represent certain qualities, good or bad, and to stand for particular philosophies or attitudes to life.

In *As You Like It*, all the main characters ultimately find themselves in the Forest of Arden. There they find refuge from the cruel court life they have left behind: 'Are not these woods / More free from peril than the envious court?' asks the exiled Duke Senior.

### Hint

The idea of 'refuge', a place where some sort of healing can take place, is a very important idea in the Pastoral.

The forest also, however, provides a space in which the characters can 'find' themselves and in which they can test the truth of their professions of love. Having learned more about themselves and the true nature of things, they can return to the court.

The pastoral world acts as a teacher. It is honest, unlike the devious characters of the courtly world. Again it is the Duke who claims that even the rough weather of the open country brings a positive benefit: 'This is no flattery; these are counsellors / That feelingly persuade me what I am'. Later he claims that the life that he and his followers now lead

> Finds tongues in trees, books in the running brooks,
> Sermons in stones, and good in everything.

As You Like It *2.1, 16–17*

*Still from* As You Like It *– in the Forest of Arden*

Thus, from this perspective, the influence and effect of the pastoral world on the main characters is purely beneficial.

## Dramatic structure

Another useful way of examining the way that the Pastoral operates within drama is to look at the structure of the plays.

Two significant aspects of dramatic structure are the endings of the plays, and the ways that the plays develop through contrast and conflict. In this context the opposition between the court or town and the country provides an important way of exploring structure.

### Activity 6

Look at the overall pattern of any play that you are studying. Working with a partner if possible, create a time line, or chart of the action of the play. Which scenes take place in the country and which in the court, town or city? Is there any significance to the pattern? Look closely at the opening and closing scenes of the play.

The section below considers these questions in relation to the two comedies that you have looked at in this chapter.

### *As You Like It* and *She Stoops to Conquer*

The structures of these two comedies have some similarities.

- Both plays begin with a journey to the countryside by characters from the court or town.
- At an early stage of the play central characters comment on the differences between the two worlds, providing both positive and negative views.
- The action of both plays then remains in the rural setting until the end of the play.
- This period of the play represents a relatively brief period of time – days rather than months. The action is thus concentrated and any changes that take place do so quickly. The effect of the rural environment is thus intensified.
- At some stage during the play there is a further arrival of characters from the court or town. This arrival has a significant effect on the plot.

- Following the conclusion of the action, the audience is invited to imagine the return of some of the main characters to the court or town.
- The closing speeches of the play draw attention to what has been learnt in the country. The audience is invited to assume that this knowledge will be taken back to the advantage of the society of town or court.

So in this chapter you have seen how setting can play a significant part in the structure of a play. With pastoral drama the alternation of court or town and country settings may also be important in developing some of the central themes of the play.

## An example of contemporary pastoral drama

For an experience of a different form of pastoral drama, you might explore the television plays of Dennis Potter. Potter was brought up in the Forest of Dean, a small and fairly remote rural community near the Welsh border. In one form or another, the Forest is a significant presence in Potter's work. In plays such as *Pennies from Heaven*, *Blue Remembered Hills* and *The Singing Detective*, a forest is portrayed as an innocent Garden of Eden, but a paradise within which children in particular are forced to confront the existence of evil.

Potter's plays deal with the question of guilt, especially sexual guilt; the collision between the worlds of children and adults; the enduring effect of memories of the past; and journeys of discovery within a world divided between the country and the city: all of these are familiar pastoral themes.

*Blue Remembered Hills* takes its title from a poem in the collection *A Shropshire Lad* by A.E. Housman. The poem presents a fairly conventional pastoral view of a time of lost innocence, a 'land of lost content'. Potter's play, which uses the poem as an epilogue, takes a very ironic perspective on the supposed 'happy highways' of the past.

## Commentaries

### *Commentary on Activity 2*

#### *Pastoral characters*

The countryside characters include the traditional pastoral figures of shepherds and shepherdesses. You have learnt that the pastoral genre often involves the presentation of an idealised version of a shepherd's life. A play may follow this tradition or may treat it comically.

#### *Court and country*

Those characters who are noble, or connected to the court, include (clearly) the two dukes, the 'noblemen' in attendance on Duke Senior, and the three sons of Sir Rowland de Boys, as well as Le Beau, who is simply identified as a courtier. Others are equally clearly country dwellers: Audrey is specifically described as 'a country wench', for instance. This clear division might suggest that the two groups of characters are going to be brought into significant opposition. This mixing of 'high' and 'low' characters on stage is itself a feature of Elizabethan drama that distinguishes it from earlier theatrical forms and the more classical style that emerged later in the 17th century.

#### *Connections and significance in plot*

You may have noticed that the list includes some familiar types of character from dramatic comedy. There are pairs of brothers, with some suggestion of rivalry between them. There are two daughters (of different ducal fathers) who are likely to be linked together in some way.

There are several servants, who tend to have an important supportive role in comedies. Some characters (for example, William and Rosalind) are identified as having an involvement with love or disguise, both characteristic elements of comedy.

However they are treated by Shakespeare, you may expect the shepherds and shepherdesses to be romantically involved. What you don't know at this stage is whether the two shepherds, Corin and Silvius, fulfil the same function in the play, whether they simply duplicate each other. This would not be Shakespeare's usual practice, and in fact a reading of the play might suggest that Corin (and Audrey) are more earthy creatures than the more refined figures of Silvius and Phebe. (Critics have argued that in this, and in other ways, Shakespeare's use of the Pastoral marks a reaction against the more aristocratic vision of such writers as Edmund Spenser and Philip Sidney.)

*Names and function*

The names and nature of the other country characters do suggest a comic function. 'A country wench' does not indicate the likelihood of any great sophistication on Audrey's part. 'A country vicar' may be likely to portray the comparative simplicity of rural ways; certainly the name 'Martext' ('mar' = 'spoil') does not suggest he will be much good at his job.

Some characters have been given names that derive from classical myth and legend. 'Ganymede', for instance, was Jupiter's cup-bearer, by repute the most beautiful boy ever born. Not only might this give some hint as to Rosalind's role within the play, it also illustrates pastoral writers' habit of making reference to classical literature.

### Commentary on Activity 4

Your response to the two characters' views may be affected by the order in which they appear. Mr Hardcastle is effectively offered the opportunity to comment on his wife's opinion, and you may feel his blunt good sense contrasts with her pretentiousness.

For Mrs Hardcastle, the town represents all that is sophisticated and socially desirable. It functions rather like a jeweller: it can 'rub off the rust' and give 'a month's polishing' to those who have been made dull by country living. The reference to 'rust' and 'polish' may of course also hint at a concern for rather superficial things; there's a clear sense of following the fashion here.

For Mr Hardcastle the town represents little but 'vanity and affectation'. It is the dwelling place of 'fools' who travel to the country like a plague. He makes a bitter contrast between the past and the present in this respect. Things, it seems, have got worse.

**Hint**

Reading more of the play may modify your initial view of the two characters. Mrs Hardcastle remains in many ways a deluded creature, but Hardcastle's attitudes are also subject to some comic deflation.

*Summary*

In this chapter you have explored a number of ways in which pastoral drama works. You have learnt that:

- pastoral drama is an important form of the wider genre of comedy
- the plays often feature familiar pastoral character types
- the plays often present a clash between the worlds of the town or court and the country
- the pastoral setting can make an important contribution to the plot and also help in bringing out central themes of the play
- the pastoral setting may play an important part in the overall structure of the play.

# 13 The Pastoral: different readings

*Aims of the chapter:*

- explores the idea that pastoral texts can be read in different ways, with reference to a range of contrasting texts from different periods
- considers whether the Pastoral has any relevance to the modern world
- studies examples of anti-pastoral and urban pastoral writing.

## Understanding genre

The understanding of genre can help readers by providing them with a familiar set of patterns and themes. The recognition of these features may help them to anticipate and predict what will appear in the text. In this way genre texts can offer a comforting reading experience: readers may feel that they are operating within a secure set of values that are held by society as a whole.

However, the reading you have done so far, both in this unit and in other parts of the course, will have shown you that understanding of a text is always open. Texts contain many meanings and you will have seen that they can be interpreted in many ways.

In addition, genres are not static. They evolve. What may seem to be their conventional features alter over time. Genres also seldom operate in isolation. They may compete with other genres within a text in such a way that the presence of one genre affects how we read the other.

Questions that you might ask yourself in relation to your reading of genre texts are:

- Does the existence of genre conventions tend to make you read the text in a particular way?
- Do you ever resist this suggested reading?

### Activity 1

As a way of exploring this idea that genre is not a 'fixed' form, and is subject to variation over time, look at the following extracts from pastoral texts.

These texts, which are listed chronologically, were written during different historical and literary periods. Do they seem to you to operate in significantly different ways within the pastoral genre? Look carefully at both content and use of language.

You may wish to do some background research into the texts to assist your analysis.

### Link

For a commentary on Activity 1, see the end of the chapter.

### Pastoral texts from different periods

#### *1667*

In the following extract from *Paradise Lost*, Adam and Eve are preparing themselves for their day's work in Eden. They are discussing how their work might be divided.

### 1 John Milton, *Paradise Lost*

To whom mild answer Adam thus returned.
Sole Eve, associate sole, to me beyond
Compare above all living creatures dear
Well hast thou motioned, well thy thoughts employed
How we might best fulfil the work which here
God hath assigned us, nor of me shall pass
Unpraised: for nothing lovelier can be found
In woman, than to study household good,
And good works in her husband to promote.

*Book IX, 226–34*

#### *1751*

Gray's *Elegy* deals with the idea of unfulfilled ambition, both in the case of an individual young man whom Gray knew and in the general case of the village inhabitants whose talents were never allowed a wider stage.

### 2 Thomas Gray, *Elegy Written in a Country Churchyard*

Perhaps in this neglected spot is laid
Some heart once pregnant with celestial fire;
Hands, that the rod of empire might have sway'd
Or wak'd to extasy the living lyre.

But Knowledge to their eyes her ample page
Rich with the spoils of time did ne'er unroll;
Chill Penury repress'd their noble rage,
And froze the genial current of the soul.

*Verses 12 and 13*

#### *1912*

The poet is in Berlin, and contrasts the unattractive, regimented German city with the countryside around Grantchester, near Cambridge.

### 3 Rupert Brooke, *The Old Vicarage, Grantchester*

Here am I, sweating, sick and hot,
And there the shadowed waters fresh
Lean up to embrace the naked flesh ...
Here tulips bloom as they are told;
Unkempt about those hedges blows
An English unofficial rose;
And there the unregulated sun
Slopes down to rest when day is done,
And wakes a vague unpunctual star,
A slippered Hesper; and there are
Meads towards Haslingfield and Coton
Where das Betreten's not verboten.

*Lines 19–21, 25–33*

#### Did you know?

Following his time at the University of Cambridge, Rupert Brooke moved to the nearby village of Grantchester in 1909 where he and others established an artists' colony. Brooke's early death in 1915, while on the ill-fated World War One Dardanelles expedition, helped to establish his reputation as a romantic poetic hero.

#### Language hint

**Hesper:** an evening star

**Meads:** meadows

**Haslingfield and Coton:** Cambridgeshire villages

**das Betreten:** stepping onto (i.e. walking on the grass)

**verboten:** forbidden

### *1972*

This poem suggests that England may be doomed to lose all the beauty of its rural past, buried under the advance of urbanisation.

## 4 Philip Larkin, *Going Going*

It seems, just now,
To be happening so very fast;
Despite all the land left free
For the first time I feel somehow
That it isn't going to last.

That before I snuff it, the whole
Boiling will be bricked in
Except for the tourist parts –
First slum of Europe: a role
It won't be so hard to win,
With a cast of crooks and tarts.

*Verses 6 and 7*

### *1981*

In this poem from his collection *The School of Eloquence,* Harrison contrasts the fame of William Wordsworth with the obscurity of W. Martin, the paperhanger employed to restore Wordsworth's cottage in 1891. Martin's graffiti was later discovered under the wallpaper.

## 5 Tony Harrison, *Remains*

Though thousands traipse round Wordsworth's Lakeland shrine
imbibing bardic background, they don't see
nailed behind a shutter one lost line
with intimations of mortality
and immortality, but so discrete
it's never trespassed on 'the poet's' aura,
nor been scanned, as it is, five strong verse feet.

W. Martin's work needs its restorer,
and so from 1891 I use
the paperhanger's one known extant line
as the culture that I need to start off mine
and honour his one visit by the Muse,
then hide our combined labours underground
so once again it might be truly said
in words from Grasmere written by the dead:

*our heads will be happen cold when this is found*

**AQA Examiner's tip**

It is important to recognise that genre is not 'fixed'. Like language itself, any genre undergoes modification over time.

Your reading of these extracts should have suggested to you some ways in which writers' work within the pastoral genre has changed. Remember that these changes can be driven by:

- political and social contexts
- cultural contexts
- philosophical and religious contexts
- literary fashions and movements
- the biographical context of the writer.

## Anti-pastoral and the 'death' of the Pastoral

One way in which this modification occurs is through hostile or critical interpretations of the pastoral genre. Some of these writings have been labelled 'anti-pastoral'.

The anti-pastoral view may suggest that the pastoral vision distorts reality. The life of the agricultural worker for much of our history was fairly grim, both physically and financially. A rejection of literary pastoral may also point out that the work of the farm labourer can be very boring. Instead of the passage of time, or the seasons, bringing pleasure and variety, for the real-life worker in the fields each new day might merely bring repeated forms of drudgery.

For an example of this point of view, read the following passage from *The Thresher's Labour*, by Stephen Duck, a farm worker of the 18th century. In the poem he contrasts the idealised world of courtly pastoral with the grim reality of the farm labourer's life.

> Let those who feast at Ease on dainty Fare
> Pity the Reapers, who their Feasts prepare:
> For Toils scarce ever ceasing press us now;
> Rest never does, but on the Sabbath, show;
> And barely that our Masters will allow.
> Think what a painful Life we daily lead;
> Each morning early rise, go late to Bed;
> Nor, when asleep, are we secure from Pain;
> We then perform our Labours o'er again:

***Stephen Duck**, from* The Thresher's Labour *(1736)*

## Eco-criticism

One relatively recent development in literary theory that you might find useful in your reading of the Pastoral is eco-criticism. This is a complex way of reading texts, but one of its important contributions is to assert the autonomy of nature. Nature exists independent of the ways humans choose to represent or think about it. It is not merely there to be 'used' by writers and artists. Eco-critics pay a lot of attention to the ways in which nature is represented and often explore literary texts in the context of 'factual' works about the natural world.

### Hint

The prefix **eco-** relates to ecology and the environment.

## Commentaries

### *Commentary on Activity 1*

*1 John Milton, Paradise Lost*

*Paradise Lost* has a strong persuasive element, as Milton put it 'to justify the ways of God to men'. You will have noticed how the figure of God is centralised within this extract. Milton's garden has been created by God; it therefore represents order and law.

You may also have felt that women are significantly positioned here. Eve is seen through Adam's eyes, a version of the 'male gaze' that film critics often refer to when discussing how the cinema presents women. Eve's superiority is stressed, but only in comparison with 'all [other] living creatures'. Her designated role seems very much subordinate to that of the man; however, the importance of work is stressed for both Eve and Adam.

**Key terms**

**Blank verse:** unrhymed verse, usually written in iambic pentameters (ten-syllable lines with five stresses).

**Abstraction:** not concrete, an idea.

**Lyrical:** song-like, expressing feeling.

If you have looked at the metre of this extract, you may have identified Milton's use of **blank verse** as a significant feature, along with patterned repetition of words and phrases, all contributing to the poem's solemn rhetorical effect.

### *2 Thomas Gray, Elegy Written in a Country Churchyard*

Milton's poem is in many ways about man and his relationship to God. It thus has a very significant public and religious purpose. Poets such as Gray, writing in the post-Augustan period, were more likely to see themselves as separated from, rather than a representative of, society.

Certainly there is a sense in which Gray is writing from a more personal perspective. The 'neglected spot' of the village churchyard also represents the individuals who are laid there, and perhaps also the poet himself. The extract interweaves different strands of imagery, symbols of power and creation (the 'rod' and the 'lyre'), and personification of the capitalised **abstractions** 'Knowledge' and 'Penury', together with familiar pastoral climatic metaphors: 'chill' and 'froze'.

### *3 Rupert Brooke, The Old Vicarage, Grantchester*

Rupert Brooke is usually included in the group of early 20th-century poets known as the 'Georgians', along with others such as W.H. Davies, Walter de la Mare and A.E. Housman. *The Old Vicarage, Grantchester* has many of the features normally associated with Georgian poetry: the celebration of English countryside, a direct and uncomplicated language, and a **lyrical** form. Georgian poetry has been criticised for its too easy retreat into nostalgia and its rather sentimental escapism. Do you feel that this extract has those faults? You may find some of the vocabulary (e.g. 'meads'), phraseology, rhyme and rhythm rather self-consciously poetic, and the contrasts between the German city and English countryside unsubtle. On the other hand you may enjoy the slightly wry humour and the melodic, evocative effects of the verse.

When Georgian poetry fell out of fashion, the criticism it attracted also led to a more general hostility to pastoral verse. Do you have sympathy with this view, or do you feel that the Pastoral has more to offer than what you see in this extract?

### *4 Philip Larkin, Going Going*

This poem comes from the post-war period of the latter half of the 20th century. You may have found this extract very different from the poems you've read so far in terms of its voice and vocabulary. The context seems much more contemporary. The language and voice are often deliberately down-beat, ironic and dismissive. The poetic voice is observant, but without illusion; the vocabulary is colloquial – not at all consciously 'poetic': 'snuff it', 'the whole / Boiling', 'crooks and tarts'. The poem reveals the familiar pastoral concern about time, but the perspective is rather different from that of earlier poets. Now there is a painful sense of the impermanence of things; this is a world where the forces of change are powerful, destructive and seemingly inevitable: 'For the first time I feel somehow/ That it isn't going to last.'

### *5 Tony Harrison, Remains*

You may have found something similar in the language and voice of the Tony Harrison extract. You may also have noticed a more left-wing, anti-establishment attitude.

The narrative voice of the poem switches from literary references and half-quotations ('intimations of mortality' is a nod at Wordsworth's *Ode on Intimations of Immortality*; Harrison is thinking about the nature of mortality – what survives and what doesn't), to the slightly sardonic everyday language: 'traipse round'. The poem is built around two sorts of 'literary' production. Harrison takes Wordsworth's unchallenged reputation as a 'classic', 'quality' author and balances it against an almost anonymous voice. W. Martin's one line of (non-standard English) poetry is ironically recorded (if hidden) in Wordsworth's own cottage. Harrison positions himself deliberately between the two voices: 'I use / the paperhanger's one known extant line / as the culture that I need to start off mine'.

In this poem, therefore, the pastoral poetic tradition itself comes under scrutiny. Has it become the voice of the establishment? Harrison sets out to assert the claims of the underground voices that we seldom hear.

*Summary*

In this chapter you have:

- compared texts from different historical periods
- analysed how language shapes meaning in literary texts
- considered different interpretations of the Pastoral
- developed an understanding of the significance of contexts
- learnt to use some appropriate literary terminology.

**AQA Examiner's tip**

The Summary shows how your work in this chapter has given you experience in addressing all of the Assessment Objectives. In your studies always ensure that you keep the Assessment Objectives very firmly in mind. Every examination unit will be based on them.

# 14 Preparing for the examination

*Aims of the chapter:*

- explains what you need to do to be well prepared for your examination in Unit 3.

**AQA Examiner's tip**

Always make sure that your **preparation and revision** involve a specific task, with a specific amount of time allocated and a clear end result. **Revision** involves looking over something you have done already, which is important, but it is equally important to do something new, to prepare some thoughts and ideas on topics and aspects that have not been covered so far.

**Link**

See the Introduction to this book (pvi) for an outline of the examination requirements.

**AQA Examiner's tip**

Always make sure that your focused stint of work leaves you **better informed** about the key topic – in this case Gothic or Pastoral – than you were before you started. Also make sure that you have a **written record** of what you have prepared so that you can glance over it in the final few days before the examination.

This short final chapter on Unit 3 gives you some hints on final preparation for your A2 English Literature examination – some of which apply to all your exams, whatever the subject. These hints are based on the assumption that you have worked hard up to this point and that you have read the texts and know them well.

## Using this book

One obvious way of preparing for the examination is to use this book. Take each of the chapters in turn and apply its focus to the actual set texts you are studying.

You might also, along with your teacher, think of some ways of distinguishing between the three texts you have studied for this unit. Here are some points to consider, bearing in mind that this is a closed-book examination:

- The unit is organised around each of two areas: Elements of the Gothic, and Elements of the Pastoral. This means that you do not need to know everything there is to know about these texts: your starting point for revision will be ideas about the generic area you have selected.
- Remember that in Section A of the examination you will be required to write in some detail on one of the three texts. Which text will it be? How many of the three do you intend to prepare for in this way?
- Remember that in Section B you will need to write in a much more general way about the three texts you have studied. Do you have a good overview of them, and can you recall significant parts of them without delay?
- How are you going to prepare for the fact that your answers will need to support their ideas with specific reference to the texts themselves? Section A will require fairly detailed reference, Section B more general reference. For further guidance on this see below.

## The essay

In both sections you will be required to write an essay on an aspect of your chosen genre. What in outline will this involve?

### Section A

- You will need to write a short introduction giving an overview of the topic as it affects your chosen text.
- You will need to address the question directly, answering what is required rather than what you would like to see!
- You will need to provide evidence from the text to support your arguments. The nature of the evidence will depend on the form of the text itself. If it is a poem or poems then there will be some expectation that you can quote words, phrases and sometimes whole lines to support your ideas. If it is a play, then again you may need to quote directly from speeches. If it is a novel, though, it is more likely that you will refer to the text rather than quote directly. See below for a further discussion of how to quote and refer.

- You will need to weigh up various possible interpretations of the text while at the same time developing a line of argument in your own essay.
- You will need to write a brief conclusion which summarises your ideas and the arguments you have made.

Below are some typical questions on specific texts.

## Examination-style questions

### Elements of the Gothic

1. Explore the dramatic use Shakespeare makes of occult and supernatural elements in *Macbeth*. (*40 marks*)
2. Discuss the view that Webster's main interest in *The White Devil* is not in physical horror but in psychological depravity. (*40 marks*)
3. Many critics have commented that the 'creature' is ultimately a character with whom we sympathise. Explore Mary Shelley's presentation of the 'creature' in *Frankenstein* in the light of this comment. (*40 marks*)

### Elements of the Pastoral

1. Consider the view that, in *As You Like It*, Arden is conceived as a place of refuge from the evils of civilisation. (*40 marks*)
2. 'In *Songs* Blake clearly locates the corruption of human social and spiritual values within an urban and industrial environment.' Discuss the validity of this view with reference to appropriate poems.(*40 marks*)
3. Potter's play *Blue Remembered Hills* has been described as 'a complete rejection of the myth of childhood innocence'. To what extent would you agree with this verdict? (*40 marks*)

Notice here that although the questions focus on an element of the Gothic or Pastoral genre, you are still expected to show your understanding of other aspects of literary study, many of which were developed during your AS course. So, for example, writing about your chosen text as an example of a play, a novel or a poem will also be very important.

## Section B

- You will need to write a short introduction giving an overview of the topic as it affects your chosen text.
- You will need to address the question directly, answering what is required rather than what you would like to see!
- You will need to check carefully the extent to which the questions ask you to compare your texts or just to write about them. If asked to compare, you will need to ensure that you do some cross-referencing of the texts – but you do not have to keep doing this all the time. If asked to write about the topic, you do not need to compare texts, but you might occasionally choose to do so. Remember that the texts have already been connected by being placed in the generic category you have been studying.

- You will need to provide some evidence from each of the three texts, but with limited time you cannot be expected to refer to everything.
- You will need to write approximately the same amount on each text, but there is no rule that says they have to be exactly equal.
- You will need to tie your ideas together at the end with a brief conclusion.

You will need to practise this sort of writing.

Below are some typical questions.

## Examination-style questions

### Elements of the Gothic

1. To what extent do you think that the presence of the supernatural is an important feature in gothic texts? *(40 marks)*
2. Explore some of the ways in which writers generate a sense of fear or terror in their gothic texts. *(40 marks)*

### Elements of the Pastoral

1. Discuss the uses made of urban and rural oppositions in pastoral texts you have studied. *(40 marks)*
2. To what extent is a pastoral treatment of the past inevitably nostalgic? *(40 marks)*

**AQA Examiner's tip**

At some points in your preparation programme, actually write some full sample answers and show them to your teacher for feedback and guidance. There is no substitute for this experience and any revision programme that does not include plenty of writing practice is bound to be limited in its effectiveness.

Notice that in this section the questions are inevitably more general in terms of their reference to texts, but they are still tightly focused on key ideas as to how the gothic/pastoral genres work. This means that in answering these questions you really must do precisely as the question asks. It is very helpful to practise how to read a question and how to break it down into its constituent parts.

## Learning to quote and refer

How are you going to prepare for giving textual evidence? One form of evidence is direct quotation, and you are far more likely to use this with poetry and drama than with prose fiction.

### Quotation

Quotation can involve quoting chunks of text, but it can also involve integrating words or phrases into your own syntax. So while you could quote from *Paradise Lost* by writing:

> Milton begins his poem with his narrator describing the content of the poem:
> 'Of man's first disobedience, and the fruit
> Of that forbidden tree, whose mortal taste,
> Brought death into the world'

You could also write:

> In his opening lines Milton's references to 'disobedience' and 'death' immediately show the gothic nature of the poem.

The second method is often better as it lets you get on with your argument while at the same time showing that you know the text well. Practise this method of quoting and you will soon find that you become adept at it.

### Reference

Equally effective, and at times even more effective, can be reference. Reference is when you show awareness of an event, a character, a place etc. by referring to it with knowledge rather than using the exact words the author uses. Keeping for the moment to the lines above, if you refer to them you would write something like:

> Milton's references at the start of the poem to moral failure and its mortal consequences immediately introduce us to gothic possibilities.

Reference has particular value when you are dealing with novels, where direct quotation can be difficult in a closed-book examination.

To summarise, here is a list of points to bear in mind when you are using quotation and reference:

- You should support your arguments with frequent and relevant textual evidence.
- Quotations should be brief.
- Quotations should be accurate.
- The best quotations are embedded in your own sentences.
- Reference to the text can also help to give evidence: close references can often work better than quotation.
- Quotations and references should never stand alone: they should be used in support of specific points you are making.

## The examination itself

By the time you take the Unit 3 examination, you will be something of a veteran of exams with lots of previous experience to draw on. It is certainly worth looking back on exams you have done well in and trying to remember what it was that made the difference.

Nonetheless, if you are well prepared then exams should be seen, in part anyway, as a chance to show what you know – it should not be beyond possibility that an examination might even be an enjoyable experience.

Senior examiners are often asked what are the hallmarks of students who write good answers. Here are some qualities of students who do well in English Literature:

- They give relevant ideas presented accurately.
- They write about the texts in a non-chronological way, highlighting the key points straight away.
- They understand the significance of authorial techniques.
- They use their knowledge of the texts selectively.
- They give the impression they are enjoying what they are doing.
- They argue a case from beginning to end.
- They are open-minded while having their own opinions.

So doing well is nothing to do with luck – it's all about preparation in advance, and calm performance on the day. By A2 these two qualities should be achievable.

#### Hint

As a general rule, short concentrated bursts of work, followed by periods of relaxation, are much better than long stretches of time which deliver little in terms of end product.

#### AQA Examiner's tip

The very highest marks usually go to students who give the impression that they are thinking about the topic rather than repeating what they have said before. Among all the pressure of the event itself, try to find time to think clearly and write with precision.

UNIT 4

# Further and independent reading

## Introduction to Unit 4

*Aims of the chapter:*

- provides information about the basic unit requirements including number of texts you must read
- considers the significance of the words 'further' and 'independent'
- encourages students to conduct an audit of personal reading so far in the course as a whole.

**AQA Examiner's tip**

Whether or not you use a text that you have used previously should ideally depend upon whether it offers you an interesting task, and whether you can pursue an interest in the text that you have already established but not had the chance to write about.

### Assessment of Unit 4

This unit will be assessed by the production of a coursework portfolio of two pieces of work. These are:

1 A comparative study of an aspect of two texts of your own choice (1,500–2,000 words).

2 The application of an aspect of the pre-released critical anthology to a text of your choice (1,200–1,500 words).

Although it is highly likely that the first piece will be submitted in the form of an academic essay, there is more scope for freedom in the written genre you use in the second part. In responding to the critical material you could, for example, write a piece of polemic journalism, although it is worth remembering that your mark for the piece will be awarded on the quality of your literary response.

### How many texts must I read?

In the whole A Level you must read a minimum of twelve texts. At AS you have already read six, and for Unit 3 you have read at least three. This means that Unit 4 requires you to read three more texts.

There is, however, a detail that needs to be explained here. The pre-released critical anthology counts as one of your texts, and is compulsory. This means that you need to read two more new texts to make the number up to twelve, even though you will actually be writing in your coursework about three. The logic of this is clear: if you wish, one of the texts you write about in Unit 4 you can have studied and written about in another part of the course, albeit for a different purpose.

### What is meant by 'further' reading?

The comparative term 'further' implies that you are expected to read beyond a certain point and extend your reading beyond what you have done so far. So what have you done so far, and how can it be taken further?

At AS you read six texts. You studied four of these with the primary focus of thinking about narrative, in Unit 1. You then studied another two texts in Unit 2, this time plays in the tragic genre.

In Unit 3 you have read three texts within either the Gothic or the Pastoral genre.

## Activity

As you start thinking about your work for Unit 4, it is time to do an audit of your reading so far, and consider some of the possible ways you can take your reading further. The audit could take the following form and will take some time to research. You will then also need to put aside time to read the further texts. The information you require will be available from a number of sources, including literary reference books (see opposite for a selection), the internet and, of course, your teachers.

1. Make a list of the texts that you have read so far and connections you have made across them.
2. Are there any texts which you especially enjoyed? If so, find out about other texts by the same author and consider reading one of them.
3. Is there an aspect of one particular text that you have studied which you have not written about, but would like to? This could be the one text you are allowed to use again.
4. Which genres/topics have you found most interesting? What other texts are worth reading in this genre?
5. Are there any genres or topics that this course has not covered, but in which you are interested? What texts are worth reading in these areas?
6. Do you have one or more favourite texts, not available on this course, that you would like to write about?
7. What pairs of texts could work well together in the comparative part of this unit?

Possible sources of reference in book form are listed in the margin. They are a small selection of the many general books on literature that are available.

## Further reading

**Reference sources**

Carter, R. *The Routledge History of Literature in English: Britain and Ireland*, London: Routledge, 2001

Cox, M. *A Dictionary of Writers and Their Works*, Oxford: OUP, 2001

Drabble, M. *The Oxford Companion to English Literature*, Oxford: OUP, 2006

Head, D. *The Cambridge Guide to Literature in English*, Cambridge: CUP, 2006

Marcus, L. *The Cambridge History of Twentieth-Century English Literature*, Cambridge: CUP, 2004

Parini, J. *The Oxford Encyclopedia of American Literature*, Oxford: OUP, 2004

## What is meant by 'independent' reading?

There is a requirement that by the end of the course you are doing some work that is independent. There is also a requirement that coursework is different from examinations – which means that the types of task are different, and that not everybody in a group is doing the same thing.

The ideal scenario in Unit 4 is that as much as possible is done independently. This does not mean, though, that you are left to your own devices. The work that you do independently, both the initial reading and then the writing, should be monitored by your teacher(s).

AQA Specification B takes a realistic view of what is possible. For example, some students are taught in small groups where personal supervision is straightforward and manageable. Others are taught in much larger groups where it is not always feasible for one teacher to supervise an unlimited range of reading and tasks.

Another issue also needs to be addressed in Unit 4 – that is your own ability and ambitions in this subject. For some students who are very able, totally free and independent work is straightforward; for others it is much more of a struggle.

All of which means that there is no single answer to the question posed at the start of this section – which should be seen as helpful to you and your teachers. However, in the two parts of this unit you should be aiming to do as much as is possible on your own, supported and encouraged by your teachers but not spoon-fed by them. This should then mean that you get the chance to work on what you are interested in, and have the satisfaction of knowing that much of what you have done is very much your own work.

# 15 Comparing texts: a checklist

*Aim of the chapter:*

- introduces one of the two pieces that will make up your A2 coursework folder, a piece that involves comparing and contrasting some aspects of two texts of your choice.

## Key terms

**Compare:** to look at two or more texts and find significant similarities between them.

**Contrast:** to look at two or more texts and find significant differences between them.

**Intertextuality:** the ways in which texts connect to each other. This can range from explicit reference to more implicit suggestions. So Stephen Fry's book *The Ode Less Travelled* makes an explicit reference to a poem by Robert Frost, while a crime story that uses forensic techniques at its centre is inevitably linked to other stories which do the same.

**Sub-genre:** a specific category within a less specific one. For example, the forensic crime novel is a sub-genre of crime fiction.

**Satire:** writing that aims to ridicule and expose human vices and weaknesses. It often uses irony, parody and exaggeration to achieve its effects.

## AQA Examiner's tip

When asked to *compare and contrast* in a question you are being asked to do two things.

## Compare and contrast: why do it?

The first thing you need to understand is that although the words **compare** and **contrast** often appear together, they have importantly different meanings. Comparison, as used here and more widely in academic contexts, involves finding aspects of *similarity* in texts. Contrast, on the other hand, involves finding aspects of *difference*.

The requirement that you show a comparison/contrast between texts in this unit is not an arbitrary one – it is not just another hoop to jump through. It is in fact a logical extension of what you have been doing in the other units.

In Unit 4, however, there is a specific requirement to *compare/contrast* two texts of your choice. This comes in A2 because it throws light on the reading process as a whole and is a reflection of what we all do as readers. That is, we process a new text by consciously or subconsciously relating it to all the other texts we have read and processed in our lives. It should be clear, therefore, that all our reading is **intertextual** and that it is inextricably tied up with notions of **genre**.

## Genre and sub-genre

As you will already have seen in previous units, the word genre has a number of different applications within the study of literary texts. On the one hand it refers to very broad definitions of types of text: poetry, prose and drama. On the other hand the word 'genre' refers to much more specific categories of texts such as tragedy or Gothic or Pastoral. But because tragedy is itself too broad a term for some of the specialised type of tragedies written, **sub-genres** are constantly being identified: these include revenge tragedy, social tragedy, tragedy of the common man, etc.

Who is it, though, who 'identifies' these genres, who suggests that texts be linked together through category? In short, all those who have a vested interest in the text. Authors often see themselves working within genres; readers identify a product that they know they like and which lives up to certain expectations; and publishers can build up their sales by trading on what they know is commercially successful.

## Similarity and difference

As we have already seen, the two key factors that determine the way we categorise texts are *similarity* and *difference.* All of the following can be seen as similarities through which genres are created and so are likely to lead to useful ways of comparing/contrasting two or more texts:

- similarity of *formal* arrangement (e.g. a sonnet)
- similarity of *content* (e.g. crime fiction, science fiction)
- similarity of *narrative method* (e.g. first person, unreliable narrative)
- similarity of *intended audience* (e.g. designed for a specific age group)
- similarity of *intended response* (e.g. tragedy to make you think, comedy to make you laugh, **satire** to make you consider the world around you)

- similarity of *occasion* (e.g. written for weddings or funerals)
- similarity of *time* (i.e. written in the same period of time)
- similarity of *production* (i.e. written by members of a distinct group of people, although they may not think of themselves as a group at the time)
- similarity of *authorship* (e.g. Shakespeare standing alone: we study 'Shakespeare').

When choosing texts to consider for Unit 4, the starting point will usually be that the texts have something in common.

### AQA Examiner's tip

If your point of connection between two texts involves the fact that they are similar in content, that they are apparently 'about' the same thematic topics, remember that your essay will nonetheless be assessed against all four Assessment Objectives.

### Activity 1

This activity does not replicate your coursework essay, because the texts are far too brief for that, but it will highlight some of the processes you will go through as you make your choices of the texts to pair together and the issues you would wish to pursue.

The following texts are all similar in that they portray figures who at the time of writing were powerful. For each one a short introduction is given, to place it in context.

Read the texts carefully and then answer the following:

1. Is it possible to find a connection linking all these texts, beyond the fact that you have already been told they are about powerful people?
2. Decide which pairs of texts can be compared/contrasted and for what reasons. At this stage come up with as many pairings as you can but bear in mind that you need to think about author's method (AO2), possible meanings (AO3) and the influence of contexts (AO4).

## Text 1

In this poem Shelley describes a form of nightmare. Castlereagh, Eldon and Sidmouth were all leading politicians of the time.

### 1 Percy Bysshe Shelley, from *The Mask of Anarchy* (1819)

As I lay asleep in Italy,
There came a voice from over the Sea,
And with great power it forth led me
To walk in the visions of Poesy.

I met Murder on the way –
He had a mask like Castlereagh –
Very smooth he looked, yet grim;
Seven blood-hounds followed him;

All were fat; and well they might
Be in admirable plight,
For one by one, and two by two,
He tossed them human hearts to chew
Which from his wide cloak he drew.

Next came Fraud, and he had on,
Like Eldon, an ermined gown;
His big tears, for he wept well,
Turned to millstones as they fell.

And the little children, who
Round his feet played to and fro,
Thinking every tear a gem,
Had their brains knocked out by them.

Clothed with the Bible, as with light,
And the shadows of the night,
Like Sidmouth, next, Hypocrisy
On a crocodile rode by.

And many more Destructions played
In this ghastly masquerade,
All disguised, even to the eyes,
Like Bishops, lawyers, peers, and spies.

## Did you know?

Castlereagh was an Anglo-Irish politician who also held the title of Marquess of Londonderry. After a colourful political career, which included having a duel with a fellow cabinet member, he eventually killed himself by cutting his own throat. Some claim that this was because he was worn down by the public abuse he received, others that he increasingly suffered from mental illness.

## Text 2

In this pretend epitaph Byron comments on the death of the politician Castlereagh.

### 2 Lord Byron, an epitaph (1822)

Posterity will ne'er survey
A nobler grave than this:
Here lie the bones of Castlereagh:
Stop, traveller, and piss.

## Text 3

*Gulliver's Travels* describes the fictional journeys of Lemuel Gulliver through various strange places. Here Gulliver describes his experience at the court of the King of Lilliput. The Lilliputians are a mere six inches tall.

Gulliver's Travels

### 3 Jonathan Swift, from *Gulliver's Travels* (1724)

The Emperor lays on the table three fine silken threads of six inches long. One is blue, the other red, and the third green. These threads are proposed as prizes for those persons whom the Emperor has a mind to distinguish by a peculiar mark of his favour. The ceremony is performed in his Majesty's great chamber of state, where the candidates are to undergo a trial of dexterity very different from the former, and such as I have not observed the least resemblance of in any other country of the old or the new world. The Emperor holds a stick in his hands, both ends parallel to the horizon, while the candidates, advancing one by one, sometimes leap over the stick, sometimes creep under it backwards and forwards several times, according as the stick is advanced or depressed. Sometimes the Emperor holds one end of the stick, and his first minister the other; sometimes the minister has it entirely to himself. Whoever performs his part with most agility, and holds out the longest in leaping and creeping, is rewarded with the blue-coloured silk; the red is given to the next, and the green to the third, which they all wear girt twice round about the middle; and you see few great persons about this court who are not adorned with one of these girdles.

*Part 1, Chapter 3, pp74–5*

## Hint

The 'former' trial of dexterity which Gulliver refers to is rope-dancing, used to select candidates for high office at court.

## Text 4

In this verse letter Pope writes to an old friend about his life as a poet. In this extract he describes Sporus, who is generally taken to be the politician Lord Hervey.

### 4 Alexander Pope, from *Epistle to Dr Arbuthnot* (1735)

Let Sporus tremble – 'What? that thing of silk,
Sporus, that mere white curd of ass's milk?
Satire or sense, alas! can Sporus feel?
Who breaks a butterfly upon a wheel?'
Yet let me flap this bug with gilded wings,
This painted child of dirt that stinks and stings;
Whose buzz the witty and the fair annoys,
Yet wit ne'er tastes, and beauty ne'er enjoys,
So well-bred spaniels civilly delight
In mumbling of the game they dare not bite.
Eternal smiles his emptiness betray,
As shallow streams run dimpling all the way.
Whether in florid impotence he speaks,
And, as the prompter breathes, the puppet squeaks;
Or at the ear of Eve, familiar toad,
Half froth, half venom, spits himself abroad,
In puns, or politics, or tales, or lies,
Or spite, or smut, or rhymes, or blasphemies.
His wit all see-saw, between that and this,
Now high, now low, now Master up, now Miss,
And he himself one vile antithesis.
Amphibious thing! that acting either part,
The trifling head, or the corrupted heart,
Fop at the toilet, flatt'rer at the board,
Now trips a lady, and now struts a lord.
Eve's tempter thus the rabbins have express'd,
A cherub's face, a reptile all the rest;
Beauty that shocks you, parts that none will trust,
Wit that can creep, and pride that licks the dust.

### Did you know?

Hervey was a courtier and politician who served both the monarchy and the prime minister, Walpole. A number of writers attacked him for this, seeing him as a sycophant and a traitor. He was not averse to replying in kind, though, mocking Pope for his deformity.

### Language hint

**Rabbin** is a now rarely used word for rabbi.

## Text 5

This novel takes as its starting point the imaginary fact that the UK is now a republican state and that the royal family, Charles and Camilla, have been exiled to a very ordinary street.

### 5 Sue Townsend, from *Queen Camilla* (2006)

Somehow, the fact that he had chosen a red washing-up bowl felt significant to him. Perhaps, as Laurens Van Der Post had urged, he was finally getting in touch with the 'pagan inside'. He and the long-dead guru had trekked across the Kalahari and sat by a campfire under a vast star-filled sky and talked of what a man needed in order to feel complete in himself. A man must have a passion, they had concluded. Charles remembered the crimson ball of the sun as it sank behind the dunes. Perhaps this metaphysical experience had influenced his choice of washing-up bowl.

Camilla asked, 'How much was your lovely red bowl, darling?'

> Charles said a little tetchily, 'I *did* say, I bought it from the "Everything A Pound" shop, darling.' He blushed, remembering the scene when he had asked the morbidly obese shopowner, Mr Anwar, the same question.
>
> Mr Anwar, irritable after a row with his wife about the Kit Kat wrappers she had found under his bed, said in his public school accent, 'Tell me, sir. What is the name of my shop?'
>
> *p3*

## Text 6

In this novel, a ghost writer is hired to write the memoirs of the recently retired Prime Minister, Adam Lang. Here Lang is interviewed for the first time by his ghost writer, who narrates the story. In the novel there are many similarities between Lang and Tony Blair.

> ### 6 Robert Harris, from *The Ghost* (2007)
>
> 'The first thing that strikes me', I said, bringing a chair round from behind the desk so that I could sit facing him, 'is that you aren't really a politician at all, in the conventional sense, even though you've been amazingly successful'. This was the sort of tough questioning I specialised in. 'I mean, when you were growing up, no one would have expected you to become a politician, would they?
>
> 'Jesus no', said Lang. 'Not at all. I had absolutely no interest in politics, either as a child or as a teenager. I thought people who were obsessed by politics were weird. I still do, as a matter of fact. I liked playing football. I liked theatre and the movies. A bit later on I liked going out with girls. I never dreamed I might become a politician. Most student politicians struck me as complete nerds.'
>
> Bingo! I thought. We'd only been working for two minutes and already we had a potential opening for the book right there:
>
> *When I was growing up I had no interest in politics. In fact I thought people who were obsessed by politics were weird.*
>
> *I still do ...*
>
> *p81*

### *Commentary on Activity 1*

The overarching connection across all these texts is that they are to some degree *satirical*. This means that the portraits of powerful people are less than flattering; they are being presented as powerful yet open to criticism. Finding an overarching concept can be a useful starting point in choosing which texts to compare, but then it needs to be narrowed down further.

It is relatively easy to find pairs of texts that have obvious similarities. Texts 1 and 2 are about the same person, 3 and 5 are about types of royalty, 5 and 6 were written at much the same time, 1 and 4 are poetry, 2 and 4 are very hostile towards their subject, and so forth. While these are useful starting points they do not necessarily have the potential for a fuller analysis.

Because we have already found the similarity – that all the texts are satirical – a more fruitful way of finding a good pair to focus on might be to now consider difference as well as similarity. The AOs mentioned above might be accessed more sharply by finding contrasts in some key areas.

So, for example, if we take texts 1 and 6 we can say:

- Both are satirical portraits of politicians.
- Text 1 is in the form of a poem, text 6 a novel (AO2).
- Both texts have an element of fiction in the way they present the central characters: text 1 is in the form of a recalled nightmare, text 6 has a number of layers of fiction at work (AO2).
- Neither text 1 nor text 6 is a direct attack on anyone, but 1 is much less ambiguous in its approach than 6 (AO3).
- Although both texts are written about well-known politicians of their time, the satire attacks different political targets. Text 1 is about a morally corrupt group, text 6 is about a man's desire to have a good public image (AO4).

Clearly with full texts at hand (including more than just the one poem by Shelley) and so scope for reference and detail (AO1), it would be possible to build a sustained analysis of two texts which as a starting point have something in common but which then diverge in significant ways.

### Activity 2

It is likely that you have found a different pair or pairs to focus on. Now draw up a scheme similar to the one above, on another pair of texts. Developing a critical mind-set which lets you see potential similarity and difference between texts will be useful throughout your A2 course.

Note that there is no commentary with this activity. Instead the next chapter shows how you can move from an outline scheme to a fuller piece of writing, looking this time at texts 3 and 5 in more detail.

*Summary*

In this chapter you have been shown some of the many ways in which texts can be compared and contrasted, so that you can begin to look for suitable texts for your own comparative piece of coursework.

# 16 Comparing texts: an example

*Aims of the chapter:*

- introduces some of the ways in which texts can be compared/contrasted by looking at further extracts from *Gulliver's Travels* and *Queen Camilla*
- considers some of the skills and approaches you will need to show in this part of Unit 4, with a view to simulating as far as possible the processes you need to go through in planning and writing your coursework essay.

**Remember**

A **satirical** work is one that aims to ridicule and expose human vices and weaknesses.

**AQA Examiner's tip**

Examiners are often asked by students how much knowledge they are expected to assume their reader (the examiner) holds. It is a very subtle question, and there is no absolutely right answer, but in this part of Unit 4 you should assume your reader has a good working knowledge of the texts being compared.

## Reminder – what you have to do

You first have to select two texts that are suitable for comparison and contrast. You then have to arrive at a task that allows you to fulfil the various requirements already indicated in the previous chapter. The initial impulse to compare these two texts is generated by the fact that they are both satirical works.

The extended extracts below should be seen as representative samples of the two texts. In reality, of course, you would focus on whole texts, although you would still need to find for yourself suitable parts of each text for closer study and reference.

## The two extracts

### Extract 1

This extract is taken from Part 2 of *Gulliver's Travels*, entitled 'A Voyage to Brobdingnag'. Gulliver, who is presented by Swift as a rather naive narrator, has left behind the tiny people of Lilliput and is now in the land of the giants, Brobdingnag. This reversal of size means that he is now the equivalent of a Lilliputian in this world. Gulliver is summoned by the King and told to explain to him how the politics of Britain work. Gulliver begins by boasting of the wonderful country he comes from, before the King gives a very different version of it.

***Gulliver's Travels*** **(1726)**

I began my discourse by informing his majesty that our dominions consisted of two islands, which composed three mighty kingdoms under one sovereign, besides our plantations in America. I dwelt long upon the fertility of our soil, and the temperature of our climate. I then spoke at large upon the constitution of an English Parliament, partly made up of an illustrious body called the House of Peers, persons of the noblest blood, and of the most ancient and ample patrimonies. I described that extraordinary care always taken of their education in arts and arms to qualify them for being counsellors born to the King and kingdom … To these were joined several holy persons, as part of that assembly, under the title of Bishops, whose peculiar business it is, to take care of religion, and of those who instruct the people therein. These were searched and sought out through the whole nation, by the Prince and his wisest counsellors, among such of the priesthood, as were most deservedly distinguished by the sanctity of their lives and the depth of their erudition …

That the other part of the Parliament consisted of an assembly called the House of Commons, who were all principal gentlemen, *freely* picked and culled out by the people themselves, for their great abilities, and love of their country, to represent the wisdom of the whole nation …

I then descended to the Courts of Justice, over which the Judges, those venerable sages and interpreters of the law, presided, for determining the disputed rights and properties of men, as well as for the punishment of vice, and protection of innocence. I mentioned the prudent management of our Treasury, the valour and achievements of our forces by sea and land. I computed the number of our people, by reckoning how many millions there might be of each religious sect, or political party among us ... And I finished all with a brief historical account of our affairs and events in England for about an hundred years past ...

His Majesty, in another audience was at pains to recapitulate the sum of all I had spoken ... then taking me into his hands and stroking me gently, delivered himself in these words '... you have made a most admirable panegyric upon your country. You have clearly proved that ignorance, idleness, and vice are the proper ingredients for qualifying a legislator. That laws are best explained, interpreted and applied by those whose interest and abilities lie in perverting, confounding and eluding them ... by what I have gathered from your own relation, and the answers I have with much pains wringed and extorted from you, I cannot but conclude the bulk of your natives, to be the most pernicious race of little odious vermin that Nature ever suffered to crawl upon the surface of the earth.'

*Part 2, Chapter 6, pp167–73*

Gulliver's Travels

## Extract 2

The novel *Queen Camilla* is told in episodic short sections. This extract describes a cabinet meeting at some vague time in the near future. The United Kingdom is now a republic with the royal family exiled to an exclusion zone on a council estate. The cabinet is discussing an economic crisis.

### *Queen Camilla* (2006)

The Cabinet had been in crisis session for over six hours. Sustained only by mineral water and Rich Tea biscuits, they had been discussing the balance of payments, again. The Government had been in power for thirteen long years, having won three general elections, the last by a small majority. Introducing the Exclusion Zones had won them short-term popularity, but water rationing, hospital closures and monumental mistakes by Vulcan – 13,000 paediatricians had been erroneously placed on the paedophile register – had resulted in the pound faltering and falling like a novice ice skater.

The Chancellor was saying to his exhausted, and in some cases tearful, colleagues, 'I warned you that losing the cigarette duty would leave a big financial hole. We have to find another source of revenue.'

Jack Barker, who had been kept awake half the night listening to the Chancellor's dog, Mitzie, yapping through the party wall, said, 'There's plenty of disposable income out there. If the taxpayer can afford bloody aromatherapy candles and grooming products for men, they can afford another tax. I reckon we ought to bring dog licences back.'

There was general laughter. Even the Chancellor smiled.

Jack waited for the laughter to die down, then said, 'There are too many dogs in this country. Did you know there's six million one hundred thousand of them? Or that people spend over three billion quid on feeding the spoilt bastards? And four hundred million a year on buying the flea-bitten hairy-faced ball-lickers Christmas presents. *Four hundred million!*'

The Chancellor looked down and shuffled his papers. Last Christmas he had bought Mitzie a pink latex bone, and a hairbrush and comb set. He'd had them gift-wrapped, at Harrods.

Jack continued, 'And did you know that their combined turds, if laid end to end, would go to the moon and back twice?'

Jack had made this last statistic up, but he had no conscience about the fabrication. After years in politics he knew that statistics were statistically unreliable.

Neville Moon, Home Secretary and owner of two excitable chocolate Labradors, said, 'Prime Minister, you can't touch dogs, not in this country. Not in England!'

Jack said, 'I propose we charge three hundred quid a dog.' Looking at Moon he said, 'No make that five hundred.'

The Deputy Prime Minister growled, 'It's political suicide, Jack. You might as well jump off the top of the fucking Gherkin.'

Mary Bush, Health Minister and owner of a trembling greyhound, said tentatively, 'It has been shown in various studies that dogs have a beneficial effect on the old and the lonely.'

Jack said, looking directly at Mary, 'Do you know how many kiddies go blind every year because of the *Toxocara canis* worm found in dog shit? After waiting a few minutes he answered his own question. 'Three,' said Jack, dramatically holding up three fingers.

Bill Brazier said, 'Three? Is that all?'

'Bill, that's three little kids who will never see their mother's face. Never see the wonder of spring blossom on a ...' Jack's mind went blank. He couldn't remember the name of a single tree. So he went for the generic, '... tree,' he finished.

Jack said, 'I want reports on my desk this time tomorrow. Costs to the National Health of dog bites and kids going blind, etc. Costs to the police of dog-related incidents, costs to the fire service of dog rescues. The bleedin' things are always falling down wells and mine shafts. I want to know how many tonnes of carbon monoxide emissions are caused by transporting dog food around the bloody country. I want television campaigns. I want billboards. I want dog owners to be the next lepers. We did it with smokers, we can do it with bloody dogs.'

*pp50–2*

## Starting the essay: making notes

One obvious way to begin the process of writing a comparative essay is to make preliminary notes on each of the texts. These notes will focus on the sorts of things that you have been looking for throughout your course. So for each text we can make notes on the following:

1. What genre(s) are we looking at in the text?
2. What methods of writing is the author using within these genres?
3. What **contextual** matters need to be considered?
4. What potential meanings are being made in the text?
5. Is it possible to interpret the text in different ways?

### Key terms

**Contextual:** relating to **context** (as defined in the Introduction to this book); the circumstances surrounding a text which affect the way it is understood and so need to be considered when we analyse it.

## Activity 1

Have a go at making notes on these two texts, using the numbered points above.

### *Commentary on Activity 1: Notes on* **Gulliver's Travels**

*1 What genre(s) are we looking at in the text?*

- One genre to note is that this is a parody of a travel book, in which an outsider gives an account of travel in a strange land, in this case the entirely imaginary Brobdingnag.
- Another genre is to do with purpose – this is a political satire on the institutions of British politics.

*2 What methods of writing is the author using within these genres?*

- The travel book genre means that the narration is in the first person, and Gulliver gives an account of his interview with the King.
- The contrast between what Gulliver proudly says about his own country, and what we as readers actually understand, is the effect of an ironic method of presentation.
- If we are in any doubt of the real significance of what Gulliver tells the King, then the King's reply allows Swift to make the satirical points clear.
- This narrative method means that while Gulliver might see things one way, as readers we can be aligned in other ways – here perhaps much more with the king.

*3 What contextual matters need to be considered?*

- As ever with context we need to decide which is most important and how much to use. In terms of contexts of production we might consider: (1) Swift's personal position as an Irish Tory at a time of Whig rule – in other words he has personal scores to settle; (2) the rather different power structures than we have now, with Monarchs and Lords carrying more power than they do now.
- More importantly, though, we can consider contexts of reception – why are we still reading this book now? Above all because it looks at power, especially political power. Can we find aspects of power described in 1726 that are still present today?

**Did you know?**

Whigs were one of the two main political parties of the time – the other was the Tories.

*4 What potential meanings are being made in the text?*

- Many of Swift's satirical points become clear once we understand the **ironic** method, for example. So when he describes the 'extraordinary care' taken in the education of the nobility, we know he means the opposite, and are not in any real position to argue.

*5 Is it possible to interpret the text in different ways?*

- We can find more ambiguity of meaning in the King's final assessment that 'the bulk of your natives [are] the most pernicious race of little odious vermin …' Amongst possible interpretations here are:
  1. Swift, via the King, is putting forward a damning judgement on all mankind
  2. Because the King has only heard Gulliver's story his judgement is based on poor evidence
  3. Swift/the King are not talking about all mankind for all time, but about the Whig government of that specific time.

  Overall the satire in this extract seems 'serious' – effects are subtle rather than downright comic.

### *Commentary on Activity 1: Notes on* Queen Camilla

*1 What genre(s) are we looking at in the text?*

- One generic aspect to consider here is that this is part of a novel, with some characters entirely fictional and some 'real', in that they purport to belong to the royal family.

*2 What methods of writing is the author using within these genres?*

- The episodic nature of the novel means that each episode is contributing to a developing plot. We can suspect here that taxing dogs is going to be significant later.
- This episodic structure allows Townsend to make satirical points both within episodes and across episodes in the wider novel.
- The narrative here is third person and quite 'distant'. We hear people speak, often in very colloquial ways, but we do not get detailed thought.

*3 What contextual matters need to be considered?*

- Because the novel is so contemporary, contexts of production and reception merge. Are we meant to see this as the Labour government completing its third term in 2010? Or is it more a picture of any government?

*4 What potential meanings are being made in the text?*

- Meanings here are pretty transparent. They also echo current events, albeit with farcical exaggeration. So, for example, the obsessive use of statistics, the failure of government agencies ('Vulcan' here), the search for policy regardless of need, can all be seen.

*5 Is it possible to interpret the text in different ways?*

- We could look at the characterisation of the Prime Minister Jack Barker (note the surname). Is he to be sympathised with in any way? Is he just to be ridiculed?

  Overall the effects in this extract seem obviously farcical and comic rather than especially subtle.

## Thinking about comparison

Once you have made your notes, the next thing to do is to look for areas of comparison (similarity) and contrast (difference).

### Activity 2

Either using your own notes, or the notes above, what areas of comparison/contrast do you think could lead to the focus in an essay, bearing in mind that you will need to cover all Assessment Objectives?

### *Commentary on Activity 2*

There are no right answers here, but one obvious way of working is as follows.

1. The overarching comparative connection is with the idea of satire on government.
2. There are contrasting narrative methods.
3. There are contrasting contexts of production and reception.
4. Although in a broad sense there are some comparative meanings to be found, at a more detailed level the texts are working towards rather different levels of meaning and effect.

## Forming a task and title

Once you have outlined comparative/contrastive points you are ready to construct your task and title. In most cases you will do this with your teacher/tutor.

Here are some possible tasks which could arise for the work so far in this chapter.

- Compare and contrast the ways in which Swift and Townsend present aspects of power and politics in *Gulliver's Travels* and *Queen Camilla*.
- Is it fair to say that Swift is more interested in serious concerns and Townsend more interested with comedy in *Gulliver's Travels* and *Queen Camilla*?
- Swift was writing in 1726, Townsend in 2006. To what extent does their satire share common concerns and how is it different?

Note here that although all the Assessment Objectives are not explicitly addressed, it is impossible to answer these questions without writing about authors' techniques, possible meanings and possible relevant contexts. Note also how the requirement to compare/contrast is encoded within the titles themselves.

*Summary*

In this chapter you have simulated, as far as is possible in a book like this, the processes that you need to go through in order to plan and write a comparative piece of coursework.

**AQA Examiner's tip**

Although this is coursework rather than an exam question, your essay must relate closely to the title you put at the top. Your final mark will reflect the relevance of your approach, which shows the significance of getting the title right in the first place.

**Link**

For suggestions on how to go about planning and writing your assignment, see the Introduction to Unit 4 (pp87–8).

# 17 Reading critical material

*Aims of the chapter:*

- introduces some aspects of what is often called 'literary theory' and how it is applied in Unit 4
- focuses on different types of critical approach with specific reference to Philip Larkin's poem *Mr Bleaney*.

### Key terms

**Ideology:** the attitudes, values and assumptions that a text contains, and which readers are expected to share – although they don't actually have to. *Attitudes* are to do with the approach taken to the subject matter; *values* are to do with the beliefs expressed in the text; and *assumptions* are those things that are taken for granted and so do not need saying at all.

## Why read theory?

It should by now be clear that literature is **representational**. This means that it does not give a definitive view of the world that we can say is 'real' or 'true': instead it offers us versions of the world which we can, up to a point, recognise, depending of course on our own experience of the world in the first place. And because literature gives us versions, these versions must be **ideological** in that they encode various attitudes, values and assumptions.

Literature, then, is representational because it has to be. The very language we use, the words and sentences that make up the toolkit of literature, are themselves arbitrary labels for things and actions, rather than the things themselves. There is nothing in the signs on the page that make the word 'book' that has anything to do with the thing itself, beyond the fact that in the English-speaking world it is quite convenient that we all use the same word. The French, however, use the word *livre*. If language actually was what it labelled, then there could only be one world language.

The representational nature of literature was explored previously in your AS course, so the idea should not be new. We now need to take this a bit further, with a simple piece of logic. If literature is representational, giving ideological versions of the world, then literary criticism must also be ideological, giving 'versions' of texts. These versions arise out of the approaches that the critics use to analyse the texts in the first place.

English Literature is a young subject compared with many other academic areas: it is not much more than a hundred years old. As work in other subject areas, such as sociology, anthropology, philosophy etc. began to recognise that how you viewed the world depended in a sense on your own starting point, English Literature as a subject began to realise that, depending on the ideology of the critic and the critical methods used, different readings of a text would emerge. All criticism is rooted in theoretical starting points, and so to claim that you don't need theory to understand a text is itself a theoretical viewpoint!

It is worth noting here that Assessment Objective 3 for English Literature addresses this issue. When it refers to the need to explore connections and comparisons between different literary texts, informed by interpretations of other readers, it is stating that the ways in which we connect texts and the ways in which we interpret them need to take into account the different ways in which texts can be read.

## Why study theory?

It is one thing to accept that criticism comes from a theoretical starting point, but another to say that the theories themselves are worth studying. Why bother to read and consider critical material when there is all that literature to be getting on with?

One obvious answer to this is that understanding critical methods actually helps you when faced with literary texts. It gives you some frameworks to apply. It also highlights an interesting dilemma we all face when analysing a text. Should we, as critics, give a single and very strong reading of a text based upon one method which we happen to favour? Or should we weigh up various possible readings and understand the central ambiguity of texts and criticism?

Both approaches have a lot going for them. Some of the most interesting criticism, whether it be on books, film, music or whatever, is committed, controversial and full of attitude. On the other hand, criticism based on an understanding that the work of art can be seen in lots of equally justifiable ways can be just as interesting, even if it lacks the immediacy of the single approach. There is no reason, in your A2 coursework, why you cannot have a go at both methods.

Before looking in detail, in the next chapter, at what the pre-released booklet of critical material shows, it is worth giving an outline of its central topics. Broadly speaking the material is concerned with the following three types of critical approach.

### Political criticism

The pre-release material looks at two approaches which are both concerned with aspects of social power. **Marxist** criticism investigates the ways in which texts portray economic and other inequalities and the extent to which the text challenges these inequalities as something that needs to be changed. **Feminist** criticism looks at the representation of gender, and also urges us to consider the implications of inequality. Initially such criticism was especially concerned with femininity, but nowadays it tends to embrace other gender issues such as masculinity.

#### Hint

The word 'gender' is often used loosely. Strictly speaking, if you want to refer to someone as a man or a woman, you are referring to their 'sex'. If you want to consider how men and women are represented through aspects of masculinity and femininity, then you should use the word 'gender'. Using gender in both instances means the word loses its specific meaning.

### Linguistic criticism

The pre-release material looks at some of the ways in which literature presents its meanings through using comparison, especially **metaphor**.

### Moral and aesthetic criticism

Here two inter-related topics are looked at. In the first topic, the pre-release material considers whether it is possible to say that reading literature has any real purpose beyond the recreational, whether in some sense it can be said to be 'good' for you. In the second topic it considers whether it is possible to say that literary texts are beautiful, i.e. have **aesthetic** value, and if so whether it is possible to analyse such beauty.

#### Key terms

**Aesthetic:** relating to (the appreciation or consideration of) beauty.

## *Mr Bleaney*

As an introduction to working with theoretical ideas, and more specifically the pre-release material, some broad issues will be addressed by looking at the poem *Mr Bleaney* by Philip Larkin, first published in 1955.

#### Did you know?

Although a renowned poet in his own lifetime, Larkin was also a librarian, spending most of his working life in Hull.

#### Activity 1

Read the poem and note down any ideas that come to you on a first reading, including what you think the poem is 'about'. Also note down any parts of the poem you find difficult or puzzling and try to say why this might be the case.

### *Mr Bleaney*

'This was Mr Bleaney's room. He stayed
The whole time he was at the Bodies, till
They moved him.' Flowered curtains, thin and frayed,
Fall to within five inches of the sill,

Whose window shows a strip of building land,
Tussocky, littered. 'Mr Bleaney took
My bit of garden properly in hand.'
Bed, upright chair, sixty-watt bulb, no hook

Behind the door, no room for books or bags –
'I'll take it.' So it happens that I lie
Where Mr Bleaney lay, and stub my fags
On the same saucer-souvenir, and try

Stuffing my ears with cotton-wool, to drown
The jabbering set he egged her on to buy.
I know his habits – what time he came down,
His preference for sauce to gravy, why

He kept on plugging at the four aways –
Likewise their yearly frame: the Frinton folk
Who put him up for summer holidays,
And Christmas at his sister's house in Stoke.

But if he stood and watched the frigid wind
Tousling the clouds, lay on the fusty bed
Telling himself that this was home, and grinned,
And shivered, without shaking off the dread

That how we live measures our own nature,
And at his age having no more to show
Than one hired box should make him pretty sure
He warranted no better, I don't know.

***Philip Larkin***

## Commentary on Activity 1

When reading any text our first instinct is, in a broad sense, to work out what it is 'about', what its general contents are. So, in this poem, the **persona** who speaks the poem considers the significance of the room he lives in – what the room says about him as a person. He does this through remembering how he hired the room in the first place, and how the landlady who owns the room keeps talking about its previous occupant, Mr Bleaney. The persona wonders whether Mr Bleaney felt like he does, and whether or not he and Mr Bleaney share more than the fact that they have both lived in this room.

This poem, although in some ways quite modern, is over fifty years old, so not surprisingly there may be some references that need explaining. These might include such things as the 'four aways' (an option on the football pools which offered a reasonable chance of winning, but not much of a prize) and the significance of Frinton (a genteel but rather dull resort in Essex). References like these can be worked out through research and/or consulting your teacher.

A bigger puzzle, though, is where Mr Bleaney worked. In the landlady's words, he 'was at the Bodies', a shared reference between her and the persona, but one which leaves us puzzled. Could it refer to a car factory? (i.e. a body shop?) Was he an undertaker? Are we meant to find it a bit odd as a name and also a bit ominous?

### Key terms

**Persona:** the character who 'speaks' a poem, i.e. a created voice, not the voice of the author.

### AQA Examiner's tip

It is tempting to think that the voice which speaks a poem is the author's voice, but this is not the case – to some extent the voice is always a created voice. For that reason, we say the voice belongs to a 'persona'.

A different problem arises with the last two stanzas of the poem. These are not difficult because they have references that you may not get – they are difficult because of the complex **syntax** and verb tenses. Essentially the persona asks whether Mr Bleaney was aware of the potential significance of the room, implying perhaps that sometimes it is better not to know the truth about yourself.

What you have done in the activity above is usually the way any first reading of a text works. This baseline meaning is not likely to be referred to in your work – it is taken for granted – but without it you can't really apply the critical material.

You will now work on three activities, each of which will focus on ideas that are developed in your critical anthology.

## Activity 2

**People and power**

Think about the people who are presented in the poem.

1. What do we find out about them?
2. What attitudes do they hold?
3. What attitudes could we hold towards them?

## Commentary on Activity 2

The first thing to notice with this activity is the sequence of questions you are asked. This sequence could act as a model for approaching other texts from a broadly *political* starting point.

### *What do we find out about the people in the poem and the attitudes they hold?*

There are three people in the poem: two men (Mr Bleaney and the persona, whom we have assumed to be male) and one woman, the Landlady (who we know is female because she is referred to as 'her'). Both Mr Bleaney and the Landlady are seen through the eyes of the persona, so there is a sort of double narrative perspective.

*The Landlady*

The Landlady rents out a squalid-sounding room and is impressed by a very ordinary previous lodger whom she can't stop talking about. In the brief sketch of her character she seems stereotypically talkative, yet vacant. Her radio set is described as 'jabbering', for example. She might also be seen as manipulative, trying to get her new lodger to do the garden.

*Mr Bleaney*

Mr Bleaney is the only character with a name, and his name is also the title of the poem. By looking at the name alone, you can tell that the title is sending out an advance signal about this fictional man: he is bland, blank. It would come as a major surprise if this character turned out to be a heroic figure. The title leads the reader to believe that this is going to be a poem centred on Mr Bleaney, but arguably this is not the case. Yet we do find out a lot about him via the Landlady – and as expected he is a man locked into his 'habits'. His 'preference for sauce to gravy' suggests a man who makes only minor decisions, for example. There are other details too, such as where he goes on holiday – and the clinching fact that 'He stayed / The whole time he was at the Bodies'.

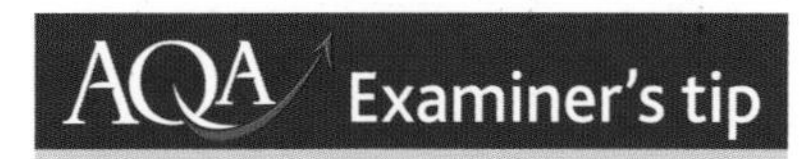


Always use evidence from the text you are analysing to support your ideas. This can be through direct quotation or through reference.

*The persona*

Least is known functionally about the persona, but he appears to be the only one who questions the set-up. He is irritated by the Landlady and her radio. And in the long final sentence covering two whole stanzas, he questions the existence he shares with Mr Bleaney and what it says about them both. He does not know whether Mr Bleaney worried about the life he led, but by implication he himself does.

*What attitudes could we hold towards them?*

A consideration of the attitudes to the characters we can hold as readers leads us to the political questions that have already been hinted at in this commentary. One way to view the Landlady is to see her as a stereotypical mixture of gossip and manipulation, in part representing her gender and its supposed attributes and in part her occupation. She could be seen almost as comic. One way to see Mr Bleaney is as a weak man, happy to accept a life of habit. He too could be an essentially comic figure. And one way to see the persona is as someone who sees more than the others do, someone who has a poetic turn of phrase ('the frigid wind / Tousling the clouds') and who at least questions his existence, even if he is not able to change it. We could see Larkin giving us a semi-comic poem about life and its routines.

A rather different way of looking at the analysis above would be more critical of Larkin. Instead of being amused by the stereotypes, it would challenge them, saying that the depictions of women (and certain kinds of men) are generalised and sneering, with the persona adopting a superior stance and looking down on the others. He lives in the room, and feigns some sort of interest in what Mr Bleaney might think, but what he is actually saying is that he is superior to them because he is more intelligent. Here you can see some ideas from feminist criticism.

A third reading is also possible, however. This time we see all three characters as much more united, because they are all locked into social roles that give them little pleasure. Each of them works: the Landlady with her shabby property she struggles to maintain, Mr Bleaney with his factory job and dull room to come home to, and the persona, whose work is not named but must be the reason he has to take the room. They are all locked in a world of alienation, driven by demands of work which tie them, and with no hope of escape. Here you can see some ideas from a Marxist perspective.

### Activity 3

**Metaphor, symbol and meaning**

Think about the significance of the room in this poem.

1. What story does the poem tell?
2. Why is the room so important to this story?
3. What broader significances can you attach to the room?

## Commentary on Activity 3

***1 What story does the poem tell?***

The story can be told briefly. An unnamed persona hires a room that was once hired by Mr Bleaney. Over time the Landlady says so much about Mr Bleaney that the persona wonders if, in some way, he is connected to the life of this very dull man by occupying the same room.

### *2 Why is the room so important to this story?*

Although the poem is entitled 'Mr Bleaney', he is never seen – it is his ex-room that is significant. This room is important because it has meaning both inside and outside the story being told; or put another way, it has literal meaning and symbolic meanings.

Within the world of the poem, the room's dreary shabbiness – evidence of which is given in some detail ('Flowered curtains, thin and frayed / Fall to within five inches of the sill') – suggests it is a bleak place in which the persona spends endless hours trying to block out the noise from downstairs. And still within the poem, the room (or 'one hired box') leads the persona to ask the long question beginning 'But if he stood and watched …' in which he wonders whether Mr Bleaney thought about what the room might say about his life.

### *3 What broader significances can you attach to the room?*

If we see only the literal meaning, we are left with a rather pointless reading experience. But if we see that the room has a potentially symbolic set of meanings then reading the poem takes on much greater purpose.

Seeing a poem as having symbolic meanings – meanings beyond the obvious, in other words – is not an unusual idea and not something that only happens in literature. We are surrounded by adverts in which a kitchen comes to represent the values of family life and security: food products, washing products, clothes etc. might all be placed in association with the kitchen to enhance the message being given. This **metonymic** association between kitchen and values is something we are used to. When we read a poem about a room, therefore, we have an expectation that the room will be more than just a literal venue.

So it is in this poem. The persona wonders whether 'how we live measures our own nature'. Note here that a poem that has been essentially about 'I' and 'him' suddenly introduces a much more inclusive 'we'. This pronoun gives a big hint to us that this poem is not just about Mr Bleaney and his room, it is about us and our lives. And of course it is not just asking us to think about the room we live in – it is asking us fundamental questions about life and choice, whether we are free or not. What you think the key words 'how we live measures our own nature' actually mean is in part down to you, as is the effect of the 'I don't know' at the end. But what should be clear is that literature has metaphor ('transferred meaning') and symbol at its heart, both in how it 'works' and in the meanings that are made.

#### AQA Examiner's tip

It is well worth knowing some of the literary terminology that is used when it comes to the broad area of comparison and meaning. **Metaphor** involves association of things or ideas because they share some similarity. A **symbol**, on the other hand, has a less obvious connection with what it is used to mean, working more by association of ideas.

#### Link

See Chapter 18 for more on metaphor and symbol.

#### Key terms

**Metonymy:** involves reference to a whole thing by either part of it or by something associated with it. For example, the UK government is often represented by No. 10 Downing Street – the building where the PM lives and the Cabinet meets. Not surprisingly metonymy is seen as very important when analysing cultural representation.

#### Activity 4

**Beauty and value**

This poem is about a bland man living in a bleak room. Consider:

1. Is it possible to say that this poem has beauty?
2. Is it possible to say that this poem offers its readers anything of value?

## Commentary on Activity 4

All the theoretical work discussed so far has stressed that such approaches open up possible meanings and interpretations, but the two questions posed in this activity would appear to work at the margins of personal response.

### *1 Is it possible to say that this poem has beauty?*

At first sight it would seem strange to suggest that a poem based on ordinary and ugly things could be considered beautiful. Some reasons for arguing that the poem gives **aesthetic** pleasure could be:

- It has a clear rhyme scheme that gives the poem an obvious sense of structure.
- However, this rhyme scheme does not constrict the poem, so that the sense can run across lines even when there are strong rhymes (e.g. the rhymes in the first stanza).
- The mixture of traditionally 'unpoetic' language with a more formal type of language could be seen as clever.
- The poem has a certain downbeat humour, especially in the way Mr Bleaney and the Landlady are represented. The use of direct speech as a form of mimicry might also appeal to some.
- The movement of the argument in the poem, from apparently trivial detail to significant question to downbeat conclusion, could be seen as unusual and so noteworthy.

From the above reasons it would seem that some sources of aesthetic pleasure come from sensual experience, in this case to do with patterns of sound, and rather more come from a sort of intellectual process – recognising the cleverness that lies in the poem, and which the poem seems to wear lightly. But these are not absolute qualities – different readers will inevitably respond in different ways, some finding other aesthetic pleasures and some not finding many at all.

### *2 Is it possible to say that this poem offers its readers anything of value?*

Again this is very much a case of individual response. At its heart this poem does seem to be doing two things which are often said to be part of literature's 'job':

- It is looking closely at the world and giving a recognisable interpretation of it.
- It is asking a fundamental question about our lives which we can apply to our own circumstances.

Put another way, this poem shows us a version of the world we can recognise and asks us to question ourselves and how we live. Some might argue that the throwaway last phrase ends the poem on a disappointing note of uncertainty. Others might argue that in wondering if others are more content than he is, the persona (and Larkin) is ending the poem asking a very subtle question.

*Summary*

This chapter has introduced you to some theoretical starting points that underpin the study of literature and help you to develop and evaluate critical approaches.

# 18 The pre-released critical anthology

*Aims of the chapter:*

- introduces some of the broad ideas in the pre-released critical anthology
- gives some ideas of how to take them further in your coursework folder.

**AQA Examiner's tip**

Remember that there is a considerable amount of freedom surrounding how you approach this material. You do not have to study it all in detail, but you should read it all at least once so that you can decide which bits in particular interest you.

**Did you know?**

Karl Marx (1818–83) was born in Germany but spent much of his life in England and is buried in Highgate Cemetery, London.

*Karl Marx*

Rather than having separate activities, this chapter does the following:

- It introduces the main topic.
- It offers a digest of each topic to be read alongside the critical material.
- It gives some suggestions for where you could find possible texts to test the material against.

Unlike other chapters, which you are likely to use in a relatively continuous way, this chapter is designed more as a reference for you to use as and when you look at different sections of the critical material.

## Section A: Political readings

### 1 Marxism

The passage from Hans Bertens on Marxism begins by making the important distinction between Marxist *politics*, which since 1989 have come to be seen as increasingly irrelevant, and Marxist *thinking*, which can still be seen as highly relevant. After all, Marx was a philosopher whose ideas were adopted by politicians, rather than a politician himself.

#### *The central ideas*

Here are the central ideas from Bertens' description of Marxism, and some of the implications that follow from them.

- Humans are not free and independent agents, acting as individuals with limitless choices. This is one reason why the **essentialist** approach to literature has to be abandoned in favour of seeing literature as **representational**.
- Humans (in this case we ourselves and the writers we read) are not separate from the **socio-economic** conditions we live under. We think and behave in certain ways because we have to. The life of the reader and the work of the author are bound together, therefore, by complex contextual connections.
- Although we like to think we live in a world of choices, this idea of choice is all an illusion – the choices we have are much more limited than we pretend.
- Because there is a gap between what we see as potential in life and what life actually offers us, we are in a sense **alienated** from the world.
- It may have crossed your mind that if we have no real choice in life, then why aren't we happy because we know nothing else anyway? Although Bertens does not say so explicitly, we can work out from what he says that the capitalist system appears to offer us choices but does not do so in reality.

#### *Possible applications in Unit 4 coursework*

From the digest above, some possible applications can be seen.

## Key terms

**Essentialism:** the belief that literature is 'real', peopled by 'real' people.

**Representational:** the opposite to essentialist, whereby literature is seen as offering highly selective versions of the world, not the world itself.

**Socio-economic:** the combination of the social and economic conditions we live under. Although the phrase always puts social first, a Marxist view would say that it is economics that determine everything else.

**Alienated:** made to feel distanced, isolated, even hostile. People can experience alienation when they feel that their lives lack full meaning because they are just part of a process.

**Sex:** the biological differences between men and women that cannot be disputed. The terms *male* and *female* also apply here.

**Gender:** the representation of women and men through cultural stereotypes. These stereotypes can and should be endlessly disputed. The adjectives *feminine* and *masculine*, and the nouns *femininity* and *masculinity*, also apply here.

*Choice and its illusory nature*

Many literary texts portray people at the crossroads, deciding which way they should go. No wonder life as a journey is such a popular metaphor (see Section B below). You could explore your chosen text to see whether choices people make in the text are 'free' or 'determined'.

Possible texts range from single poems like Robert Frost's *The Road Not Taken,* to more substantial texts such as John Milton's *Paradise Lost* or a novel by Thomas Hardy. Consider your work on tragedy in Unit 2 – tragedy is full of ideas about choices we make and the consequences of them. Your chosen genre in Unit 3 will also offer possible ideas: to what extent are ideas about choice and rebellion central to the Gothic? To what extent does pastoral literature show contentment without choice?

*The representation of social class*

To what extent does a text show individuals or groups of people locked into social roles? And to what extent does the text question the fairness of this?

Possible texts are more likely to be plays and novels, as they can explore these ideas in sufficient detail. Victorian novels and American tragic plays are obvious sources. It is possible to find poems too that give a snapshot of such ideas: Larkin's *Essential Beauty* and *The Big Cool Store* could work well.

*Alienation*

Here we can look in texts for 'outsiders', people who do not fit in, or even for whole texts that show the absurdity of a world without meaning.

Possible texts include *Huckleberry Finn*, *The Great Gatsby*, and many different types of play, including the so-called kitchen-sink dramas of the 1950s, such as *Look Back in Anger,* and absurdist plays such as *Waiting for Godot* and *Rosencrantz and Guildenstern Are Dead.* Many European writers, including some living under Communist regimes, have also written about alienation. You could, for example, look at Milan Kundera's *The Unbearable Lightness of Being*.

## 2 Feminism and gender

Feminism can be linked to Marxism in that both schools of thought see socio-economic ideas at the heart of their thinking. While Marxism sees working people as historically disadvantaged, it has traditionally failed to take much notice of another group who have been significantly disadvantaged through history, namely, women.

Marxist 'takes' on literature have tended to see how literature *reflects* the social world. Feminism, by contrast, has tended to take a stronger line, saying that literature helps to *construct* views of women that are unfair. This is why the difference between **sex** and **gender** is so important, even though the words are often confused in everyday use.

As ideas around feminism developed, it became clear that men too were potentially disadvantaged, in that they also were expected to perform within stereotypical roles that create their own problems. As gender studies have developed, they have tended to look at notions of masculinity, and the way it is represented, as well as femininity.

### *The central ideas*

Here are the central ideas from Bertens' description of feminism/gender, and some of the implications that follow from them.

- Feminists see literature as both reflecting women's lack of power and contributing to it.
- Some male authors noted for their daring depictions of the erotic have been seen by feminists as giving a very male-focused view of sex and relationships.
- Early feminists saw relationships and the wider world as operating in much the same ways: the personal is the political.
- Feminists would suggest that women need to intervene to change their social positions – so in literature they should write feminist texts.
- Women authors too have sometimes struggled to see beyond the stereotypes, because inevitably they are themselves suppressed.
- Many texts seem based on the assumption that the reader is male.
- Typically women are stereotyped either positively or negatively (from a male point of view).
- Women in positive stereotypes are seen as cute but helpless, or angelically unselfish.
- Women in negative stereotypes are seen as either seductress or shrew. Typically, therefore, passive women are seen as virtuous, active women as dangerous and selfish.
- Focus on gender shows some men in power to be dangerously weak behind their mask of masculinity.
- Our society has many attitudes, values and assumptions that are based on uncritical notions of gender. It is assumptions in particular that are dangerous, because they are not even explicitly stated. This is why feminists have been so concerned about aspects of language which seem, by their very structure, to enshrine inequality.

### *Possible applications in Unit 4 coursework*

From the digest above, some possible applications can be seen.

#### *Women and power*

Many literary texts show women as being without power. Possible texts include 19th-century novels by men such as Charles Dickens and Thomas Hardy, and more interestingly perhaps by women such as Jane Austen and George Eliot. Many novels written after 1960 represent women from a more feminist perspective. You could try novels by Fay Weldon or Margaret Atwood, for example. The play *Top Girls* by Caryl Churchill looks at women and power in an unusual dramatic way.

#### *Women and stereotypes*

Possible texts are numerous, right across the spectrum of genre and time, for example *Hamlet*, *Paradise Lost*, *Tess of the D'Urbervilles*. The novels of D.H. Lawrence, now out of fashion, and reviled by early feminists, could be possible texts, especially *Sons and Lovers*. Poetry by Carol Ann Duffy and Philip Larkin could be contrasted.

#### *Gender*

Here you can look more widely at the representation of men as well as women. Possible texts include novels by Nick Hornby, the play *Look Back in Anger* by John Osborne, plays by Oscar Wilde, men and women in the novels of Ian McEwan, and many more.

## Key terms

**Metaphor:** an umbrella term for sub-branches such as **simile**, metaphor involves the comparison of one thing, action etc. with another. When seen in longer stretches of text, with different metaphors taken from the same area of meaning, this is often called **imagery**.

**Symbolism:** involves suggestion or connection between things rather than direct comparison. A symbol is often repeated or part of a bigger scheme of suggestion. A useful term to describe a single instance of connection is **metonymy**.

**Allegory:** a narrative that can be read on more than one level (perhaps a surface meaning and a meaning under the surface – like a fable). Typically an allegory involves aspects of religion, morality or politics.

## AQA Examiner's tip

Try to see your Unit 4 coursework as part of a whole course rather than separate bits. So although the suggested reading below is linked to the second Unit 4 task, it could be that the ideas generated from the pre-release material also give you ideas for your comparative piece.

# Section B: The meaning of metaphor

This section of the pre-release material looks at a linguistic aspect of literary study – the use of **metaphor** and associated ideas.

### *The central ideas*

Various sources are used in the material. The ideas here are synthesised for you.

- Metaphor involves comparison, so is opposite to the literal. (However, the literal can itself be metaphorical in origin.)
- Metaphor serves various purposes, from helping to clarify ideas (for example, science teaching) to entertainment (for example, stand-up comedy).
- However, a key feature of metaphor is to help us 'see' things more clearly.
- Creative metaphor, much valued in literature, involves the creation of a metaphor not used before. This means the reader needs to 'unpick' the metaphor – which can often be quite difficult.
- Creative metaphor allows ambiguity of meaning, which can itself add to a text.
- **Symbolism** tends to be broader in its meanings. David Lodge sees symbolism as being about suggestion rather than comparison.
- **Allegory** goes further still, with whole narratives having 'other' meanings.
- Metaphor is so powerful and all-pervasive that it affects the ways in which we conceive the world.

### *Possible applications in Unit 4 coursework*

From the digest above, lots of ideas for tasks should be possible. Here, for example, you could look in detail at the metaphorical language in a single poem or extract. The extract from David Lodge offers a good model of how a short extract can lead to a sustained analysis which delivers all the assessment objectives.

#### *Metaphor*

Here you could explore a repeated set of metaphors/imagery in a play: for example, 'seeing' in *King Lear*. Any number of poems could be studied, and you could make connections with other reading in the material. So Robert Frost's *The Road Not Taken* could be explored in both metaphorical and Marxist terms. Novels that are organised around metaphorical as well as literal journeys could work well – a good example is Kazuo Ishiguro's *The Remains of the Day*.

#### *Symbolism*

Here you could see how Arthur Miller uses stage symbols in plays like *Death of a Salesman* or *A View from the Bridge*. Tennessee Williams also uses stage symbols in his plays. Many novels contain symbolic elements, such as Joseph Conrad's *The Secret Agent*. In terms of metonymy there is a whole sub-genre of novels which have a large house at their centre, such as *Mansfield Park* or *Brideshead Revisited*.

#### *Allegory*

This will inevitably involve the study of longer texts. It is perhaps not surprising that some allegories are seen as children's books, when they also have the potential to be something more: *Gulliver's Travels*, *Alice's*

*Adventures in Wonderland*, novels by J.R.R. Tolkien, Philip Pullman, etc. could be the focus for a study, although you would need to make sure you focus on a manageable amount of text.

## Section C: Aesthetics and pleasure, art and beauty

Of the three sections in the material, this is the most abstract in that it deals with ideas about value which are inevitably hard to define. This difficulty, though, opens up a number of ways of approaching your coursework task which give you plenty of freedom to be innovative if you wish.

### *The central ideas*

Various sources are used in the material. The ideas here are synthesised for you. These ideas are meant to be thought about and challenged.

- The word **aesthetic** became used to refer to 'good taste', so in fact represented no more than an elite group's idea of what they liked.
- At the same time artists, including writers, made beautiful things and artisans made useful things. This placed beauty above usefulness.
- The legacy of the two points above is that in the study of literature there is a **canon** of 'great' texts, which is placed above popular writing and mass media.
- Some, however, see the idea of a canon as belonging to elitist notions and helping to maintain the elite group's hold on power.
- **Russian Formalists** claimed to identify aesthetic strategies – in other words they said it is possible to show how texts seek to appeal to their readers.
- In addition to claims about their beauty, texts in the canon have been said to be 'valuable'.
- Three types of value have been identified. Texts are said by some to be of value because:
  - they are complex and so offer challenges to the reader
  - they use elegant and carefully chosen language – a special sort of 'literary' language
  - their subject matter is serious, moral and philosophical so giving readers insights into fundamental ideas.
- The canon tends to be dominated by dead, white, upper-class males.
- Who gives authority to the canon in the first place? Is the very idea of a canon part of a self-perpetuating elitism?
- 'Alternative' canons have been suggested based on writers who challenge the orthodox.
- Some more modern types of criticism have focused on readers' responses, especially the pleasure to be found in reading.
- Michel Foucault claimed that the very idea of literature is meaningless, but is sustained by writers and critics in mutual self-interest. The critics fill in the gaps that the authors couldn't in the first place!

### Key terms

**Canon:** a list of texts which are said to be of particular value and so should be read by all.

**Russian Formalists:** a group of early 20th-century critics who looked at aspects of poetry, narrative etc. to see what were common 'forms' in all literature.

### Did you know?

Michel Foucault (1926–84) was a highly influential French philosopher who was interested in the manipulation of social attitudes by those in power.

### *Possible applications in Unit 4 coursework*

From the digest above, many different types of task are possible. Some ideas are listed below but these are by no means exhaustive.

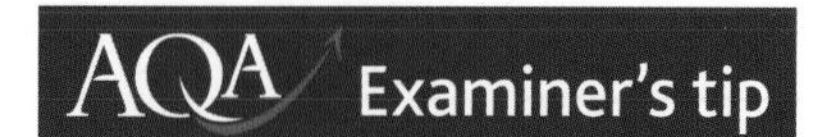

Coursework offers you the chance to follow your own interests. Showing interest in what you do will lead to a more personal response.

### Key terms

**Vernacular:** language as it is used in ordinary everyday contexts.

- You could argue the case for a text or author of your choice to be placed on an A Level set text list. You would need to make detailed reference to the text(s) and its qualities but the form you write in could be a journalistic article, for example.
- You could argue the case for the removal of a text or author from the A Level list – but make sure that your writing is based on good argument rather than mere hostility.
- You could assess the *value* of a certain text, using the criteria provided in the critical material.
- You could look at a poem or poems by writers who do not, on the surface, use 'literary language' and assess their use of the **vernacular**. Tony Harrison is an obvious modern example. Robert Burns is an 18th-century example, William Barnes a 19th-century example.
- The material suggests that comedy is often seen as having less value than more serious work. You could write a 'defence' of the *value* of a comic text you know.
- You could write about the *pleasure* that you have found in a text you have read.
- You could write about the *beauty* that you have found in a text you have read.
- The material suggests that alternative canons are based on authors who *challenge the orthodox*. You could write in support of such an author or text.

*Summary*

This chapter has introduced you to the main ideas in the pre-release critical material in order to help you work through the material and choose a suitable text and task to work on. It has been designed for reference over time rather than continuous reading.

# 19 Preparing for the coursework submission

*Aim of the chapter:*

- explains what you need to do to submit your best possible coursework.

This final chapter gives you some hints on writing your A2 English Literature coursework. It should be read in conjunction with the introduction to Unit 4 earlier in the book (pp86–7).

One obvious way of preparing for coursework is to use this book. Take each of the chapters in Unit 4 in turn and apply its content to the texts you have chosen. Consider what will be your focus in each of the two tasks. A different but equally important part of preparation involves making the best use of time given to you in tutorials.

## What is coursework?

Coursework is different from examinations. For exams, you have to prepare for all possibilities. In coursework, you can decide, with your tutor, which particular aspects of the texts you want to focus on.

Here is a reminder of what you must do in your portfolio of two pieces of coursework:

- You must write comparatively about two texts in 1,500–2,000 words. Each text should receive roughly equal treatment.
- You must apply ideas from part of the critical material to one or more literary texts.

The marking criteria for coursework are available and can help you understand what you have to do. Ask your tutor for a copy, or follow the link to the AQA website.

### Links

See the Introduction to this book for an outline of the full A2 requirements.

Go to **www.aqa.co.uk/qual/gce/eng_lit_b_new** for the marking criteria for coursework. On the right, click on 'approved specification', then on the left click on '3.4 Unit 4'.

## How should I approach the tasks?

Coursework should involve manageable tasks that can be approached sensibly. Here are some questions for you to consider, with answers given as examples of good practice. It is assumed here that you have already negotiated suitable tasks with your teachers.

### *How many pieces of work should I do?*

It is unlikely that you will do more than one comparative piece, because that involves reading two texts, but for the second piece you should certainly consider doing more than one response, so that the best can go into your portfolio.

### *How long should it take to prepare the comparative piece?*

There is no single answer here, but once you have worked out a task, your preparatory work should move fast. A tutorial with your teacher could help to establish that you are on the right lines. If having a tutorial, take your teacher some written work to see: this could be notes, an opening paragraph, a plan.

### *How long should it take to write the comparative piece?*

Not too long. Once you have finished the planning, get on with the writing or you will lose momentum.

### AQA Examiner's tip

Always make sure that your preparation and writing of coursework is well focused. Although your coursework will take time to research, plan, shape and eventually write, each stage should lead quickly to the next. Endless tinkering, and endless planning, without actually getting on with the job in hand, can lead to a stale final product.

*How many drafts should I do?*

Two should suffice. The point of re-drafting is to allow you to change the structure of your ideas; it is not to check spelling and accuracy, which is another (and much simpler) process.

*How many attempts should I have at the second task?*

Again it depends to some extent on how well you do first time, and how your teacher approaches the critical material in class. As stated above, there is no reason why you could not do more than one piece, and choose the best for submission.

*How long should I spend on the second task?*

Again you will need to do preliminary research, but with a limit of 1,500 words it should be achievable in a couple of days.

## The comparative essay

### Preparing your task (1)

After the task has been set and the tutorial taken place, get cracking, whatever the deadline might be. Putting the process off, because there is plenty of time, can be fatal. By the time you get round to it, you will have lost momentum and started to forget the text and task.

### Preparing your task (2)

Before you start writing the task you will need to organise your thoughts and sort out the references, textual and critical, that will support your ideas. You will also need to make sure that you are balancing the texts roughly equally.

In English Literature the best essays confront the task head-on. There is no need to write an introduction which says what you intend to do in your essay – just get on and do it.

So how do you decide the best sequence for your ideas? The best way is to try out different sequences in note form, and to draft different openings. When you find an opening paragraph that clearly leads on to the next ones, you are in business. Then complete your first draft quickly, giving the task your full attention.

### Writing the comparative essay

There is no single way to write a comparative essay, although as has been repeatedly stressed, relevance is vital. Clearly there are times when you need to be writing about both texts at the same time – this is especially likely when you are looking at comparison or similarity. When you are looking at difference, however, you might want to spend some time on each text separately, at the same time making it clear why you are doing this.

### How many drafts?

You may want to show your tutor a draft of your work in progress. However, you cannot expect your tutor to be endlessly looking at drafts: one full draft should be enough, especially if you have used tutorial time constructively. Your tutor can then make general comments and helpful suggestions: it is up to you what you do with these. Above all remember that coursework exists to give you the opportunity for independent study. It is your tutor's job to supervise, not to do all the hard work for you.

## Quotation and reference

Earlier in the book, you were reminded how to quote and refer in the Unit 3 examination. The difference with coursework is that you have more time to research the quotations and references you need. This does not mean, though, that large chunks of the texts should now be copied out. Exactly the same rules apply for coursework as for examinations.

Your coursework essay should present a debate and an argument. To help with this debate you can read the work of critics and then refer to it and/or quote from it as appropriate. You should reference the critics by providing the source in your **bibliography** or in endnotes.

### Key terms

**Bibliography:** list of texts you have read and then referred to or quoted from in your work.

### *Bibliographies and endnotes*

Bibliographies are usually listed alphabetically according to the author's surname. Order your entries in the following way: author's surname, author's first name or initial, title in italics, place of publication, publisher and date of publication. For example:

Conrad, J. *The Shadow Line*, Oxford: OUP, 1920
Ford, R. *A Multitude of Sins*, London: Harvill, 2001

Alternatively, you may like to use endnotes, where you include a number in the text of your essay, and reference that book at the end of it. Here are the same books, referenced 1 and 2 in the text of the essay and now giving the page number:

1. Conrad, J. *The Shadow Line*, Oxford: OUP, 1920, p34
2. Ford, R. *A Multitude of Sins*, London: Harvill, 2001, p45

## The response to critical material

Note here that the word 'essay' has not been used to describe the second task. This is because your choice of task, especially with the slightly lower word limit, might mean that you do not choose to do a formal essay. Many suggestions on tasks and activities are given in Chapter 18 of this unit, so at this point it is worth going back over that chapter. It is also worth looking again at the various writing hints given above, especially those on quotation and reference.

When preparing and then writing your task, consider the following:

- Your word limit is 1,200–1,500.
- This piece carries the same number of marks as the comparative essay.
- You need to show that you have read the parts of the critical material that are relevant to your task. You can do this by direct quotation or direct reference, but you can also do so by more implied means, provided that you show that the critical material is informing your response.

### Link

Read again the task suggestions in Chapter 18 of this unit.

## Conclusion

Coursework is included in the assessment of A2 English Literature so that you can reflect on texts and create individual responses to them. If you work sensibly, it offers the perfect balance to the demands of working under exam conditions.

# Glossary

## A

**Abstraction:** not concrete, an idea.

**Aesthetic:** relating to (the appreciation or consideration of) beauty.

**Alienated:** made to feel distanced, isolated, even hostile. People can experience alienation when they feel that their lives lack full meaning because they are just part of a process.

**Allegory:** a narrative that can be read on more than one level (perhaps a surface meaning and a meaning under the surface – like a fable). Typically an allegory involves aspects of religion, morality or politics.

**Alliteration:** the repetition, for effect, of consonants, especially at the beginnings of words.

**Ambivalent:** where one person has opposite feelings towards the same object or idea.

**Anti-pastoral:** a genre created to stand in opposition to the Pastoral, intended to subvert, to undermine the images and illusions on which the Pastoral is based.

## B

**Bibliography:** list of texts you have read and then referred to or quoted from in your work.

**Binary opposites:** a linguistic term for firmly or conventionally associated contrasting pairs in which the relationship between the two concepts is central to the understanding of both.

**Blank verse:** unrhymed verse, usually written in iambic pentameters (ten-syllable lines with five stresses).

**Blend:** a word formulation where two words are blended together; e.g. 'smoke' and 'fog' blend to form 'smog'.

## C

**Canon:** a list of texts which are said to be of particular value and so should be read by all.

**Chronologically:** in a time sequence following the order in which events occurred.

**Classical:** in the context of narrative this means traditional, based on conventional forms and a sense of order, harmony and proportion.

**Compare:** to look at two or more texts and find significant similarities between them.

**Connotations:** the implications and associations of a word (rather than the directly represented meaning).

**Context:** the circumstances surrounding a text (e.g. where it first appeared, social attitudes today) which affect the way it is understood. The word is formed from *con* (= with) + *text*, so literally it means 'what goes with the text'.

**Contextual:** relating to **context**.

**Contrast:** to look at two or more texts and find significant differences between them.

## D

**Dramatic comedy:** a play whose plot moves towards a generally happy conclusion, often involving the unravelling of a complex romantic entanglement. Comic characters tend to be of fairly humble social background (compared with those of tragedy). Comedies may be expected to provoke laughter, but the degree to which this forms the main purpose of the drama will vary considerably from play to play.

**Duplicity:** of a deceptive nature, capable of double, or multiple, meanings.

## E

**Elegiac:** from 'elegy', a lament for the dead, or for the loss of an idyllic state or experience.

**Emancipated:** freed from restraint, usually legal, social or political.

**Epic:** a long narrative – often a poem – on a heroic scale, dealing with great deeds, dangerous journeys and outsize characters. Tolkien's *The Lord of the Rings* is one example of an epic.

**Eponymous:** term applied to a central protagonist who gives their name to the title of a text.

**Essentialism:** the belief that literature is 'real', peopled by 'real' people.

**Ethereal:** heavenly, unearthly.

## F

**Feminist:** relating to the exploration and interpretation of women's experience within society (or within a text), and especially a recognition of the historical and cultural subordination of women, and the resolve to do something about it.

**Foreground:** in a piece of writing, to draw attention to something by means of a particular expression or use of language.

**Form:** the aspects of a text in its totality that enable it to be identified as a novel, or a poem, or an epistolary novel (i.e. a story told in the form of letters), or a sonnet (a poem of 14 lines), etc.

## G

**Gender:** the representation of women and men through cultural stereotypes. These stereotypes can and should be endlessly disputed. The adjectives *feminine* and *masculine*, and the nouns *femininity* and *masculinity*, also apply here.

**Genre:** a type of text (e.g. a crime novel, a narrative poem). Texts can be grouped and labelled for various reasons, such as their content, their intended audience, how readers respond to them, etc.

## H

**Hedonistic:** choosing to follow a life of pleasure.

**Homophone:** a word sounding the same as another word but spelt differently.

**Iambic metre:** a verse pattern where metrical feet consist of an unstressed syllable followed by a stressed syllable.

**Ideology:** the attitudes, values and assumptions that a text contains, and which readers are expected to share – although they don't actually have to. *Attitudes* are to do with the approach taken to the subject matter; *values* are to do with the beliefs expressed in the text; and *assumptions* are those things that are taken for granted and so do not need saying at all.

**Images/imagery:** the representation of ideas, objects and states of mind through an associated network of references.

**Intertextuality:** the ways in which texts connect to each other by referring to other texts This can range from explicit reference to more implicit suggestions. For example, Stephen Fry's book *The Ode Less Travelled* makes an explicit reference to a poem by Robert Frost, while a crime story that uses forensic techniques at its centre is inevitably linked to other stories which do the same.

**Introspective:** inward-looking, self-examining.

**Invocation:** an appeal, often to a higher power.

**Irony:** a broad term which has many different applications. Essentially irony creates effects by meaning the opposite of what it says. Inevitably, therefore, readers have to be alert to this, or they fail to get the 'real' point.

**Jacobean:** the period of the reign of King James I, 1603–25.

**Language:** (in the context of AO2) specific words or phrases in the text.

**Lyrical:** song-like, expressing feeling.

**Marginal:** on the margins, not central.

**Marxist:** there are many aspects to Marxism, but essentially it describes social change in terms of economic factors. It is especially interested, therefore, in aspects of power.

**Matriarchal:** where a mother (or mother figure) acts as the head of the family or social group.

**Metafiction:** fiction that is about fiction; stories that draw attention to their own fictional status.

**Metamorphosis:** a transformation; something or someone undergoes a change in form or appearance.

**Metaphor:** an umbrella term for sub-branches such as **simile**, metaphor involves the comparison of one thing, action, etc. with another. When seen in longer stretches of text, with different metaphors taken from the same area of meaning, this is often called **imagery**.

**Metaphorically:** not literally; an implied comparison as if the subject were something that it merely resembles.

**Metonymy:** involves reference to a whole thing by either part of it or by something associated with it. For example, the UK government is often represented by No 10 Downing Street – the building where the PM lives and the Cabinet meets. Not surprisingly, metonymy is seen as very important when analysing cultural representation.

**Myth:** a complex term, usually referring to a story that is not 'true' and deals with the supernatural and ideas of creation.

**Neo-classicism:** style in architecture and art (especially from the mid-18th to early 19th century) inspired by the models of classical Greece and Rome. 'Neo' is from the Greek word *neos*, meaning 'new'.

**Oedipus complex:** a term from psychoanalysis referring to the suppressed desire of a son for his mother or a daughter for her father, considered by Freud to be a normal part of child development. Jealousy of the other parent figure derives from these desires.

## P

**Paternalistic:** like a father; often used to suggest an excessive degree of male power.

**Persona:** the character who 'speaks' a poem, i.e. a created voice, not the voice of the author.

**Personification:** where human qualities are attributed to non-human things.

**Predator:** something or someone that preys on others.

**Protagonist:** the principal character in a narrative, often but not always the hero or heroine.

## R

**Reformation:** religious movement of 16th-century Europe to reform the Roman Catholic Church. It resulted in the establishment of the Reformed and Protestant Churches.

**Refrain:** a phrase or lines repeated at intervals during a poem.

**Representational:** the opposite to **essentialist**, whereby literature is seen as offering highly selective versions of the world, not the world itself.

**Revenant:** someone who returns (from the dead).

**Rhetorical:** using rhetoric – the art of persuasion.

**Russian Formalists:** a group of early 20th-century critics who looked at aspects of poetry, narrative etc. to see what were common 'forms' in all literature.

## S

**Satire:** writing that aims to ridicule and expose human vices and weaknesses. It often uses irony, parody and exaggeration to achieve its effects.

**Sensational:** designed merely to appeal to the emotions.

**Sex:** the biological differences between men and women that cannot be disputed. The terms *male* and *female* also apply here.

**Signify:** to convey meaning through a 'sign'; in a linguistic feature, the phrase that conveys particular meanings and associations.

**Simile:** a sub-set of **metaphor**, in which the act of comparing is explicitly drawn attention to, most frequently by use of the words 'like' and 'as'.

**Socio-economic:** the combination of the social and economic conditions we live under. Although the phrase always puts social first, a **Marxist** view would say that it is economics that determine everything else.

**Soliloquy:** a speech given by a character alone on the stage, in which they tell or confess their thoughts to the audience.

**Sonnet:** a poem that usually consists of 14 lines in iambic metre, but has a considerable variety of rhyme schemes.

**Speech tags:** words like 'he replied', indicating the speaker and the nature of the speech act.

**Structure:** how the significant parts of a text work together to form a whole, e.g. the connection between chapters in a novel, or the way time is organised, or the connection between verses in a poem.

**Sub-genre:** a specific category within a less specific one. For example, the forensic crime novel is a sub-genre of crime fiction.

**Subverted:** undermined by a particular perception or reality.

**Symbolism:** involves suggestion or connection between things rather than direct comparison. A symbol is often repeated or part of a bigger scheme of suggestion. A useful term to describe a single instance of connection is **metonymy**.

**Syntax:** the study of the relationship between words and other units within a sentence.

**Topography:** natural and man-made features of a geographical area.

**Trauma:** state of shock.

**Vernacular:** language as it is used in ordinary everyday contexts.

**Vertiginous:** tending to induce dizziness.

# Index

Entries in **bold** are key terms